Architectural Ceramic Assemblies Workshop

 University at Buffalo
Sustainable Manufacturing
and Advanced Robotic
Technologies (SMART)
Community of Excellence

 University at Buffalo
School of Architecture and Planning

Alfred University

Architectural Ceramic Assemblies Workshop

Bioclimatic Ceramic Assemblies II

Edited by

Laura Garófalo and Omar Khan

Team AECOM's glazed tiles for a scaled model to study color combinations and patterning of the Counter Current Heat Exchanger envelope system.

Contents

Team UB/Alfred's kinetic screen was constructed the first day of the workshop so that alternative assembly methods could be discussed among team members and engineering experts.

Foreword

Mic Patterson

Material and process education remains a weakness in many architectural schools, even as technological development accelerates and the building materials palette expands. Design and construction practices rooted in a rigorous understanding of materials and processes are fundamental to facilitating the transformation to resilient and sustainable buildings and urban habitat. It is critical that industry and the profession pick up the slack by providing ongoing deep, experience-based learning opportunities to students and practicing professionals alike.

The ACAWorkshop is like the playoffs of terra cotta—an ancient yet never more relevant building material—pitting world class teams of designers and makers in a friendly competitive material exploration in pursuit of innovation. The material results, as documented in this book, are compelling and significant yet are eclipsed by the experience itself; design coupled with making—rolling up sleeves and getting dirty—is a transcendent experience. Making what one designs informs the design process, which enhances the making in turn, creating endless loops of ongoing growth and refinement. The fragmented building industry often short-circuits the critical feedback loops that enable this process. Hopefully, this exemplary workshop will inspire, and act as a model for, an expanding future of industry-academic collaborations.

Kudos to the University at Buffalo School of Architecture and Boston Valley Terra Cotta on a brilliant educational collaboration and for bringing together a diverse group of designers and makers, students and professionals, providing a remarkably rich hands-on learning experience.

Team UB/Alfred's slip cast Slide Shingle awaits firing on its custom
made ceramic cradle.

In Form and Function

Omar Khan

The prototype has occupied a tenuous place in architectural design. If taken literally it refers to an original thing- idea, object, model- from which other versions or refinements are to be derived. However, in practice, if the budget allows, the prototype is relegated to the end of the design process. There in the form of a "mock-up" it can be used to problem solve the details and quality control the aesthetic intentions. Architecture unlike its sister design professions is primarily a representational practice. Prototyping in graphic design and industrial design is understood to be part of the designer's process. However, as the objects get bigger, the representations get smaller and if lucky, a scaled model is the closest an architect will get to prototyping during the design process.

The 2017 Architectural Ceramic Assemblies Workshop (ACAW) looked to challenge this reality and reintroduce the prototype as part of design thinking. This is possible if design practice and manufacturing collaborate through the design schematic and development phases. This allows for risk sharing and more importantly developing a shared intelligence. The results are better designs and less uncertainty in the execution of a construction. Boston Valley Terra Cotta as the sponsor of the workshop in association with the Sustainable Manufacturing and Advanced Robotics Technology (SMART) Community of Excellence at the University at Buffalo has looked to introduce new methods and material knowledge to the profession. The workshop serves as a means to test these ideas and consider their long-term viability in practice.

In 2017, ACAW invited three teams from the profession, AECOM, Morphosis and Walter P Moore, and one team from academia composed of architecture and ceramic arts faculty from the University at Buffalo (UB) and Alfred University. Their task was to develop architectural terracotta designs that would address the thermal, hydrological, luminesce and environmental performance of a building design. Terracotta's material properties and assembly methods were be the means to enhance the building's bioclimatic capacity to better respond to its environment.

The teams brought designs at different stages of development to the workshop. The AECOM team used the opportunity to materially explore a design they had been developing for a few years. The Morphosis team was interested in exploring manufacturing techniques and the viability of terra cotta for a speculative project in an arid climate. The Walter P Moore team took a structural approach to explore post tensioning terra cotta for unitized screen designs. And the UB/Alfred team developed shingle and tile systems that could generate complex assemblies focused on luminescence and thermal performance. For each team the prototype occupied a different part of the design process. For some it was to begin a design experiment and others to conclude and resolve a design problem. The prototypes' material presence and the reality of their manufacturing opened up many important questions that could not be addressed through models or simulations. As buildings become increasingly more complex with greater parameters to consider, the prototype would seem to be a necessary tool in the designer's expanding toolkit.

Team AECOM consulting with Boston Valley CEO John Krouse on refining fabrication of their components.

Team Walter P Moore explore threading their units to create a unitized system.

Team AECOM testing the thermal heat gain and heat transfer on their prototype.

Potential bioclimactic performances for Team Morphosis' panels are explored though sketches.

The light quality on a patterned surface studied through Team UB/
Alfred's Flip Shingle prototype.

Erik Verboon of Team Walter P Moore discussing assembly options and the potential of the glazed and unglazed surface of their units.

Participants

Bioclimatic Ceramic Assemblies 2018

Organizers

Omar Khan
Department Chair and Associate
Professorm Department of Architecture
Co-leader in the Sustainable Manufacturing
and Advanced Robotic Technologies
Community of Excellence (SMART) at
the University at Buffalo (SUNY)
Co-founder, Liminal Projects

John B. Krouse
President and CEO
Boston Valley Terra Cotta

Bill Pottle
Director of Business Development
Boston Valley Terra Cotta

Mitchell Bring
Adjunct Research Professor at the UB
School of Architecture and Planning

Speakers

Mic Patterson
Director of Strategic Development for
Schüco-USA, the Ambassador of Innovation
& Collaboration for the Façade Tectonics
Institute, and PhD candidate at the
University of Southern California

Gerd Hoenicke
Director Consulting International Projects
and Pre Construction Services at Schüco
International KG

Craig Mutter
Design Principal at CannonDesign

Dr. William Carty
John F. McMahon Professor and Chair of
Ceramic Engineering at Alfred University

Dr. Krishna Rajan
Erich Bloch Chair and Empire Innovation
Professor in the Department of Materials
Design and Innovation, School of
Engineering and Applied Sciences,
University at Buffalo

Anne Currier
Ceramic artist
Professor emerita, Alfred University

Participants

Marty Augustyniak
Façade engineer, Walter P Moore

Mitchell Bring
Adjunct Research Professor, UB School of
Architecture and Planning

Flavio Borrelli
Architect

Cory Brugger
Architect and Engineer, Morphosis
Architects

Noah Burwell
Senior Associate with Walter P Moore

Graham Clegg
Associate Principal at STUDIOS
Architecture

Christine Dunn AIA
Principal Architect at Sasaki Associates

Laura Garófalo
Associate Professor at the School of
Architecture and Planning at Buffalo
Co-founder, Liminal Projects

Matt Gindlesparger
Product Development Manager, AECOM
and Assistant Professor at Thomas Jefferson
University

Jason Green
Artist and Visiting Assistant Professor, New
York State College of Ceramics

Barry Ginder
Senior Project Designer at Granum A/I

Shay Harrison
CEO of EcoCeramics Envelope Systems

Charles D. Jones
Principal, One to One Design
Faculty at Tulane School of Architecture

Marco Juliani
Job Captain at Gensler Architects

Alexander Kellum
Visual Artist

Alex Korter AIA, RIBA, LEED AP BD+C
Associate Principal at CO Architects

Brett Laureys
Principal with Wiss, Janney, Elstner,
Associates, Inc.

Irene Martin
Senior Building Envelope Physicist at Arup

Heath May AIA
Associate Principal and Director of HKS
Laboratory for INtensive Exploration

David Merlin AIA, LEED-AP
Principal at One to One Design
Adjunct lecturer at Tulane School of
Architecture

Shawn Murrey
Adjunct Professor and Technical Specialist
for the Ceramic Art Department at Alfred
University

Chris O'Hara
Engineer and Founding Principal of Studio
NYL

Zac Potts
Designer, HKS
Lecturer at the University of Texas at
Arlington

Andrew Pries
Production Manager at Boston Valley Terra
Cotta

Casey Reas
Media Artist and co-creator of Processing
programing language
Professor of Design Media Arts at the
University of California, LA

Peter Schmidt
Information Technology at Boston Valley
Terra Cotta

Joshua G. Stein
Co-director of the Data Clay Network
Professor of Architecture, Woodbury
University

Matt Stephenson AIA, LEED AP
Senior Associate, Woods Bagot's New York
studio

Stan Su
Director of Enclosure Design at Morphosis
Architects

Erik Verboon AIA
Co-Founder and Managing Director of
Walter P Moore

Jason Vollen AIA
Principal and Director of High Performance
Buildings at AECOM, Chief Operating
Officer of Fresh Air Building Systems LLC,
and cofounder of EcoCeramics Envelope
Systems

Kelly Winn PhD
Lecturer at Rensselaer Polytechnic Institute
Architectural Researcher with the Center
for Architecture Science and Ecology
(CASE)

Han Zhang
Façade Engineer at Arup

Linda Zhang
Boghosian Faculty Fellow at Syracuse
University School of Architecture

Assistants

Frank Kraemer
Graduate Student, University at Buffalo
School of Architecture and Planning

Zach Fields
Graduate Student, University at Buffalo
School of Architecture and Planning

Evan Glickman
Graduate Student, University at Buffalo
School of Architecture and Planning

Yasmiry Hiciano
Graduate Student, University at Buffalo
School of Architecture and Planning

Blake Kane
Graduate Student, University at Buffalo
School of Architecture and Planning

Matt Kreidler
Boston Valley Terra Cotta

Richard Krouse
Boston Valley Terra Cotta Intern

Quincy K
Graduate Student, University at Buffalo
School of Architecture and Planning

Grant Landreth
Graduate Student, Alfred University

Jelani Lowe
Graduate Student, University at Buffalo
School of Architecture and Planning

Robert Miller
Boston Valley Terra Cotta

John Wightman
Graduate Student, University at Buffalo
School of Architecture and Planning

Analyzing assembly of components through direct engagement with prototypes.

Team Morphosis locating points for the attachment system.

Laura Garófalo consulting with Dr. William Carty about glazed and unglazed surface qualities.

Architects and ceramic artists collaborate on alternative surface
designs for the interior face of Team AECOM's heat exchanger.

Barry Ginder consulting with facade engineer Gerd Hoenicke about panelization and assembly methods for Team UB/Alfred.

ACAW was housed at the UB School of Architecture and Planning's fabrication workshop.

Propositions

Counter Current Heat Exchanger Using Terra Cotta Envelope Components

Team AECOM

Jason Vollen (coordinator), Flavio Borrelli, Anne Currier,
Matt Gindlesparger, Evan Glickman, Shay Harrison,
Richard Krouse, Brett Laureys, Shawn Murrey, Kelly Winn

The objective of this project is to understand how exterior terra cotta panels can be used to transfer heat to interior storage or radiator systems in buildings to reduce energy usage. Historically, heat transfer in architecture is one directional. You look to use the building's skin to maximize heat gain when it's cold outside, or lose heat when it's hot. However, heat is trying to go back and forth even as we try to control that flow. This project counters this preventive stance by adding complexity to the building surface in order to allow bidirectional heat exchange within the wall system.

The goal is to reduce peaks and valleys of heat transfer through the building envelope, and shifting them to off peak times. Very simple principles, like using a bright white ceramic with the high solar angle to reflect as much heat as possible in the summer or a dark collection surface in the winter to collect as much heat as possible, are applied. As a result rather than having a building that is constantly collecting, or losing heat, you're using that system to take that heat energy and redistributes it around the building.

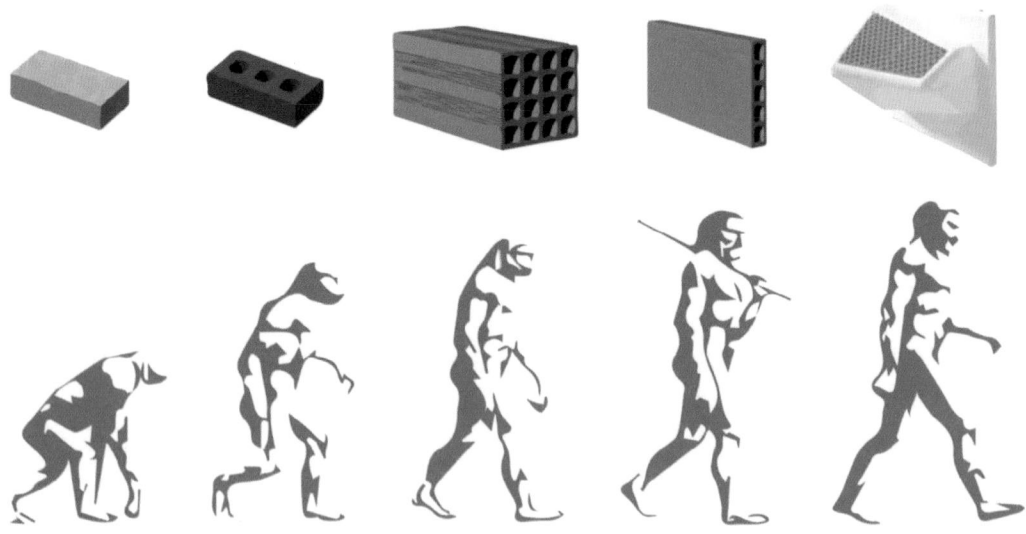

Figure 1. The evolution of terracotta components from the hand-packed brick, through volu-
metric extrusions and rain screen panels to the
thermally active heat exchange system.

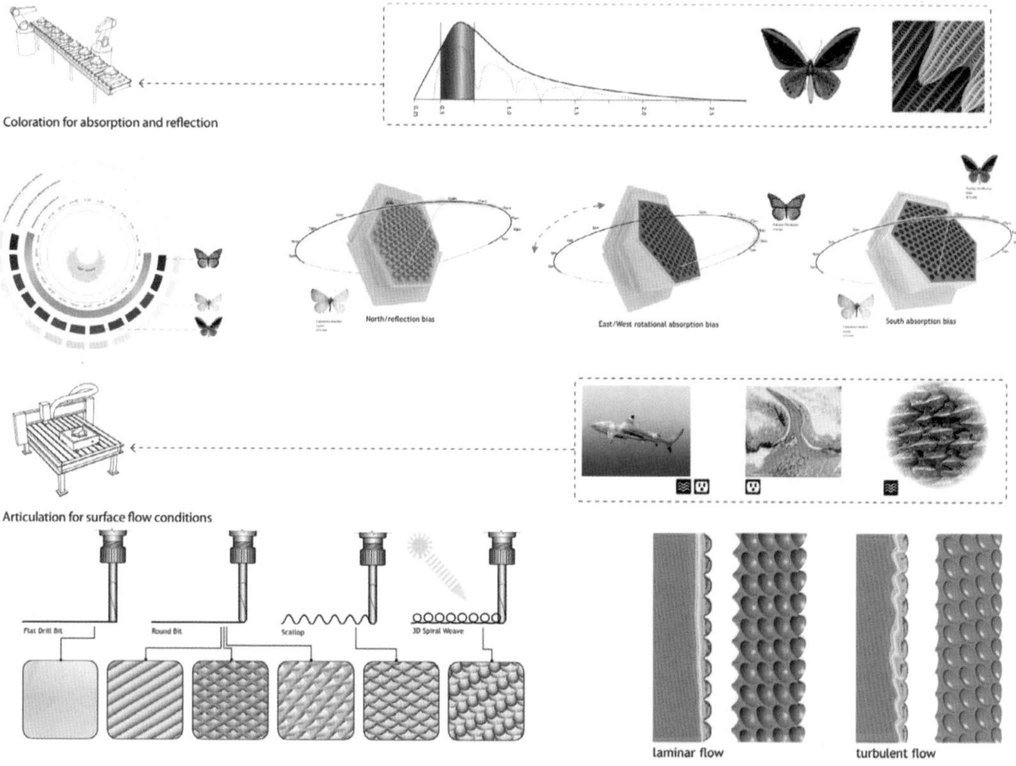

Coloration for absorption and reflection

North/reflection bias

East/West rotational absorption bias

South absorption bias

Articulation for surface flow conditions

Flat Drill Bit

Round Bit

Scallop

3D Spiral Weave

laminar flow

turbulent flow

Figure 2. The biomimetic exterior surface
takes cues from shark skin and butterfly wings
to alter air flows and maximize light energy
absorption.

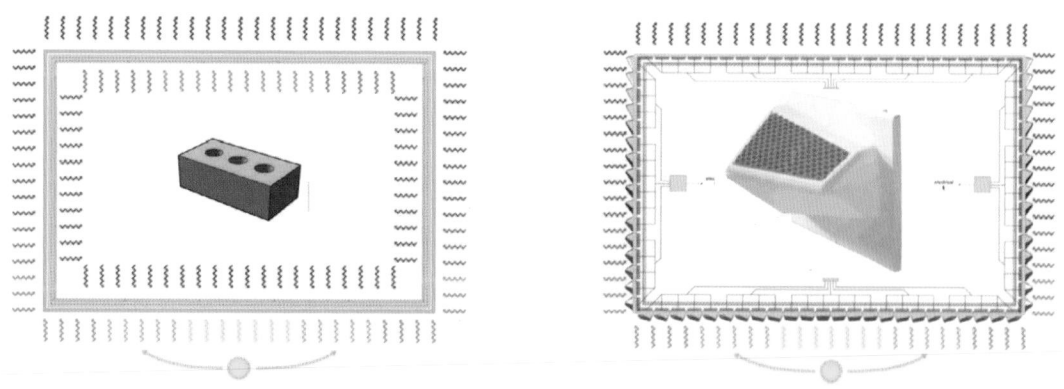

Figure 3.The design aims is to capture, trans-
form, store and redirect energy flows with the
building envelope.

There are three main components to the system.

The exterior face tile is an architectural cladding tile set to an optimal solar angle with an articulated search surface to help increase the solar collection (Figure 1); the heat exchanger takes collected heat and redistributes it into the cavity on the back of the tile (Figures 2 and 3); and the radiator enclosed in the interior panel, loops the solar heated water through its fins to heat or cool the building interior (Figure 4). The components are sandwiched together leaving an air cavity between the solar collection tile and the radiating tile. The whole facade would be plumbed in that cavity.

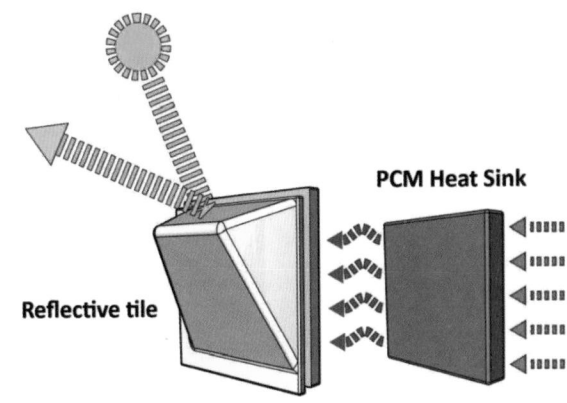

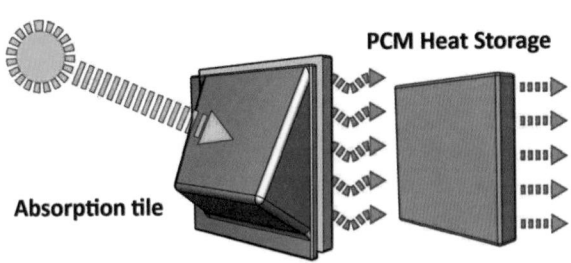

Figure 4. The design incorporates strategies that respond to seasonal change and demonstrate energy and performance gains over planar modern façade systems.

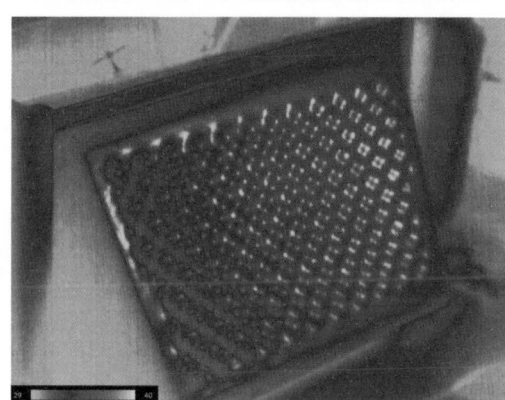

Figure 5. The exterior panel of the heat exchanger absorbs solar heat and radiates it into the cavity where fluid flows.

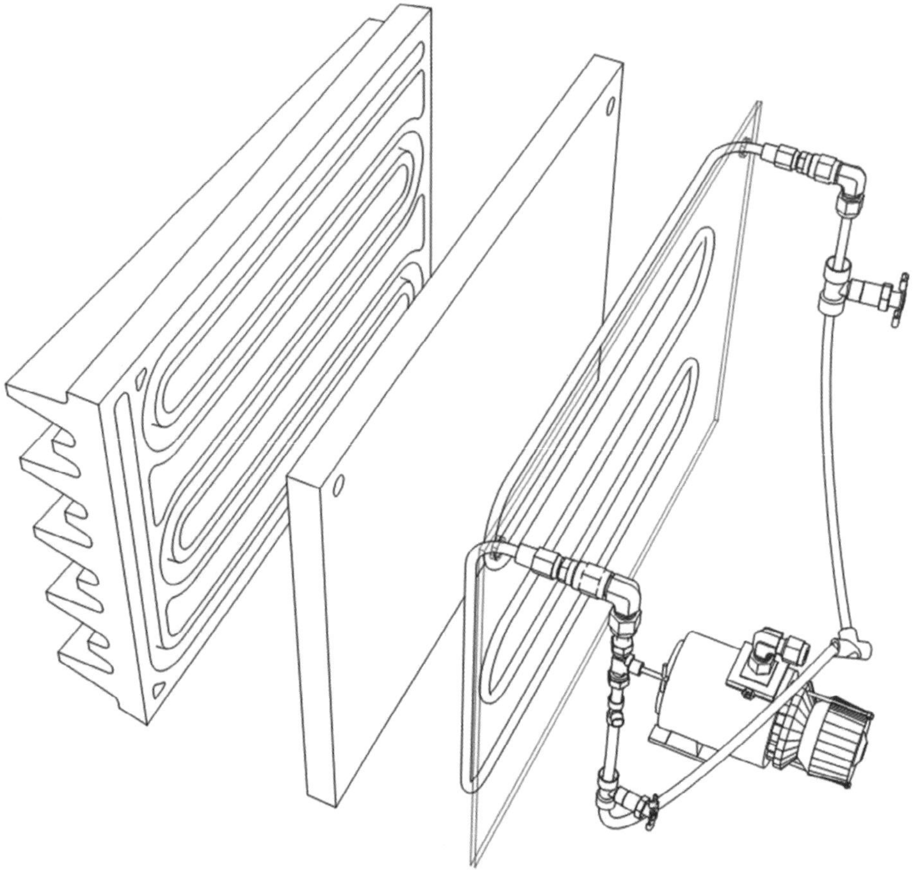

Figure 6. The assembly of the internal "radiator" panel brings together the ceramic component and the fluid loop.

At ACAW 2017 the team put together a functioning system with the components produced for us by Boston Valley. They ran some preliminary tests using a ceramic radiant heat lamp to simulate solar heat. The thermal imagery shows how the articulated surface of the solar collection tile catches the heat from the lamp and uses it to heat up the tile. After 45 minutes to an hour, they ran the fluid loop to show the heated water being circulated off the face tile into the reservoir. They were able to demonstrate that they can increase the temperature of the water when they circulate it into the radiator tile, and then distribute that heat to the building interior (Figures 5–8).

Figure 7. The team assemble a working prototype
to test its thermal storage capacity.

Figure 8. The assembly tested for its performance on heat absorption and heat retention.

Their investigation looked to combine five elements, heat exchange, color, morphology, surface texture and art in order to explore the potential of the system. Ceramic artists on the team focused on what the system could look like arrayed on a building. How does color, light and shadow effect the façade? Before the workshop, the profile of the prototype designed for optimal solar access was digitally traced and milled at one-third scale to produce a ceramic extruder plate so the unit could be produced at various lengths. By changing the length of the unit, the joints can be offset to create a more dynamic pattern where light and shadow move across the facade in different ways. The group used the scaled components produced by Boston Valley to generate multiple combinations (Figure 9–10).

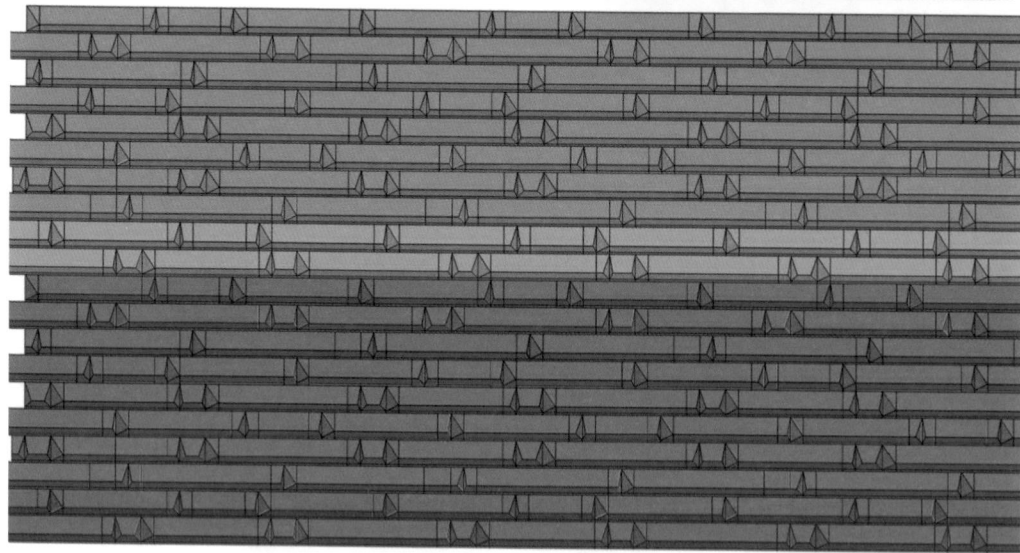

Figure 9. Potential organization of heat ex-
changers on a facade was explored in relation
to color and varying lengths of the components
using scaled prototypes.

The next step was to manipulate the extrusion itself by mitering the ends (Figure 11). The team investigated how two miter angles - forty-five and sixty degrees - come together to form a larger pattern. Although the prototype was slip cast, the need to vary the length of the panels made extrusion a good choice for production and fit well with the team's goal to explore different production options with Boston Valley to reduce fabrication costs.

Figure 10. A jig was made to test alternative miter angles for the scaled extrusions.

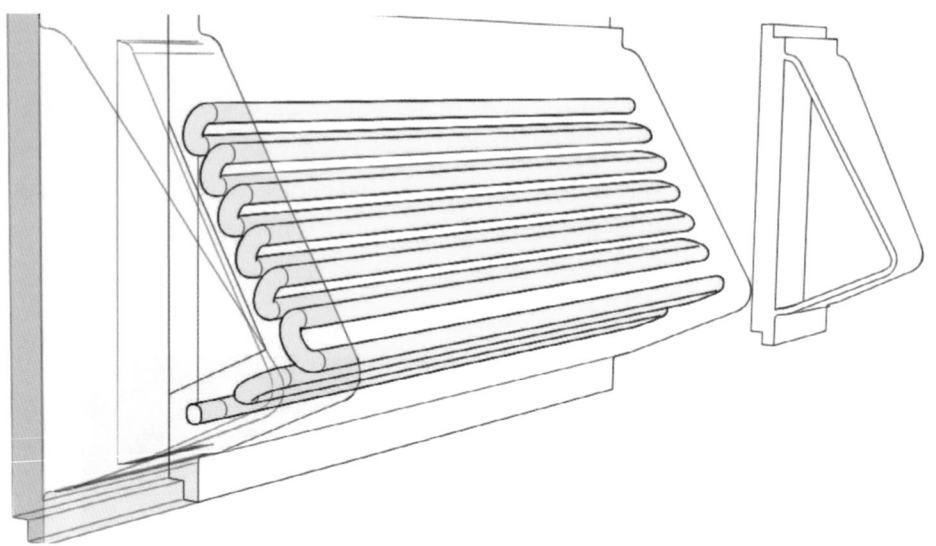

Figure 11. Extruded green-ware used to develop
the design of maintenance access caps on the
panels.

Other issues of concern were the need to service the units from inside and outside. To give accessibility for maintenance they looked at using ram-pressed end caps coupled with the extruded form. The cap would be an architectural feature and create an access panel for maintenance. During the workshop, the team worked directly with the clay as well as digitally to design these end caps that allow us to have access to the fluid (Figure 11).

The team started to introduce piping within the fired panels and planning for the extrusions to have large enough openings to run piping through them. How to we make those connections to run this through a full building façade remains to be further explored.

The radiator has the opportunity to become an artistic component of the system. It collects the heat coming from outside and channels it inward. Because this surface comes in contact with users, the team wanted to explore solutions that were friendlier, dynamic, and perhaps had a hand crafted or organic expression (Figure 12).

The team has been developing this thermally active facade system for a number of years through the Center for Architecture, Science and Ecology (CASE) at Rensselaer Polytechnic Institute, as well as NEXUS in New York and the Green Technology Accelerator Program, and now with Boston Valley Terracotta.

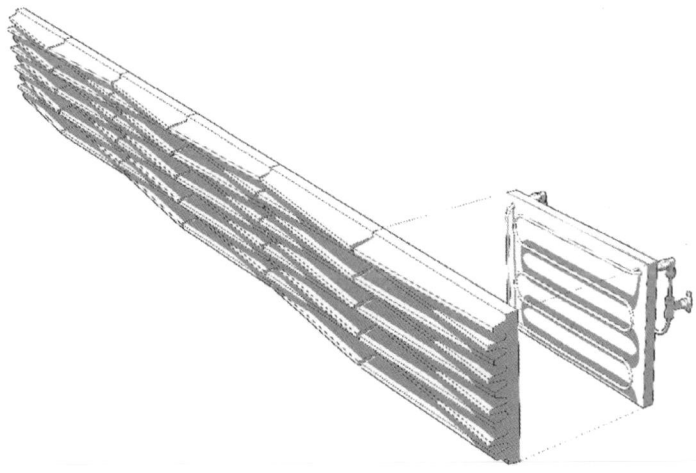

Figure 12. Rendering of the ceramic radiator.

Jason Vollen leading the discussion about the assembly of Team AECOM's prototype.

Post-Formed Ceramic Skin

Team Morphosis

Cory Brugger, Christine Dunn, Han Zhang, Charles Jones, Blake Kane, Irene Martin, Heath May, Dave Merlin, Robert Miller, Chris O'Hara, Zac Potts, Andrew Pries, Peter Schmidt, Stan Su (coordinator), John Wightman

Team Morphosis used a speculative building design with a complex form (Figure 1) to study a set of issues pertaining to the fabrication of terracotta parts. The building's shape shifts from overhung to sloped back surfaces and has both double curvature and flat portions (Figures 2, 4, and 13). The rain screen system developed to clad this surface was comprised of a series of ribbons and the challenge was how to fabricate those using manufacturing techniques for terracotta panel. The investigation had the team exploring tooling and manufacturing processes, material properties and their effect on bioclimatic design.

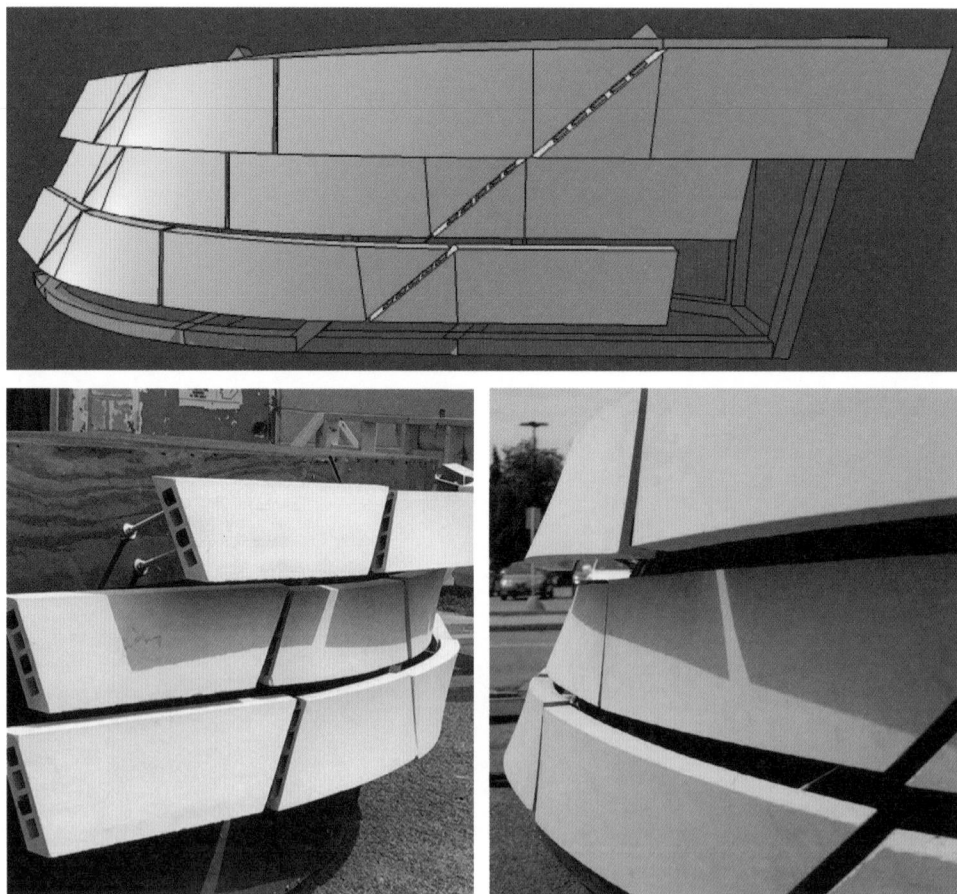

Figure 1. Design and assembly of twisted panel prototypes.

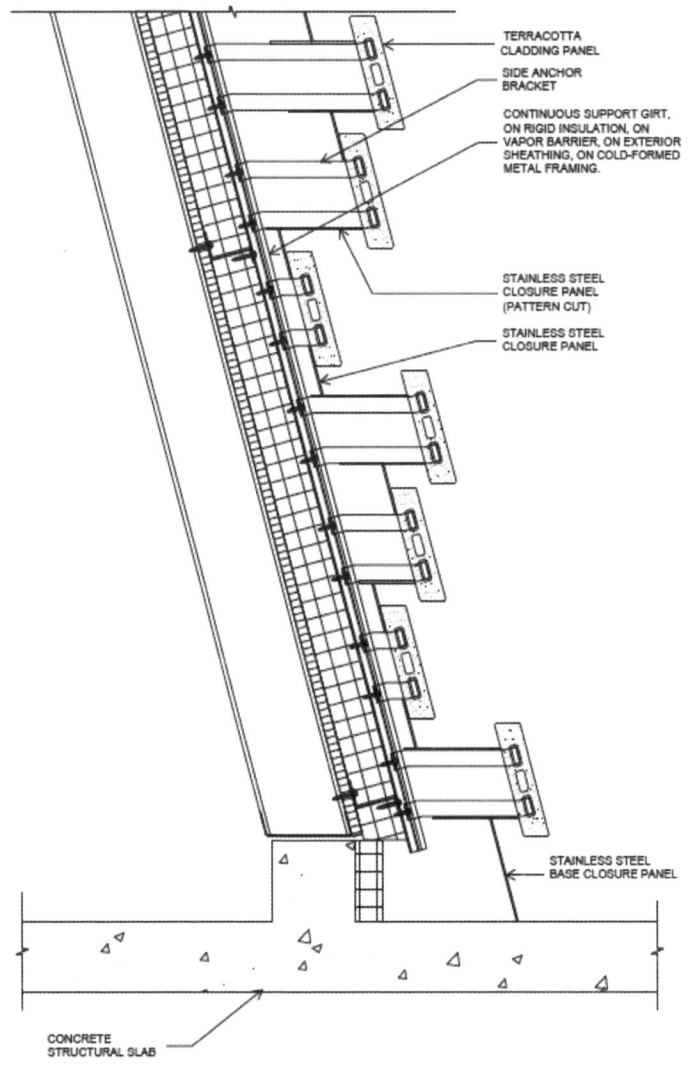

TERRACOTTA
CLADDING PANEL

SIDE ANCHOR
BRACKET

CONTINUOUS SUPPORT GIRT,
ON RIGID INSULATION, ON
VAPOR BARRIER, ON EXTERIOR
SHEATHING, ON COLD-FORMED
METAL FRAMING.

STAINLESS STEEL
CLOSURE PANEL
(PATTERN CUT)

STAINLESS STEEL
CLOSURE PANEL

STAINLESS STEEL
BASE CLOSURE PANEL

CONCRETE
STRUCTURAL SLAB

Figure 2. Wall section of rain screen assembly
showing how they cantilever off the structural
support.

The team informed their design with explorations that ranged from digital process, to fabrication techniques, and assembly detailing. They looked at the standard forming and attachment systems that Boston Valley has developed and tried to come up with an efficient way to achieve the multiple curved forms. Tooling for efficient production meant using existing industrial processes and looking at how to adapt them in the service of creating a continuous geometry. With Boston Valley, they were able to explore ways to manipulate the clay body throughout the different stages of fabrication towards their design intent (Figure 3).

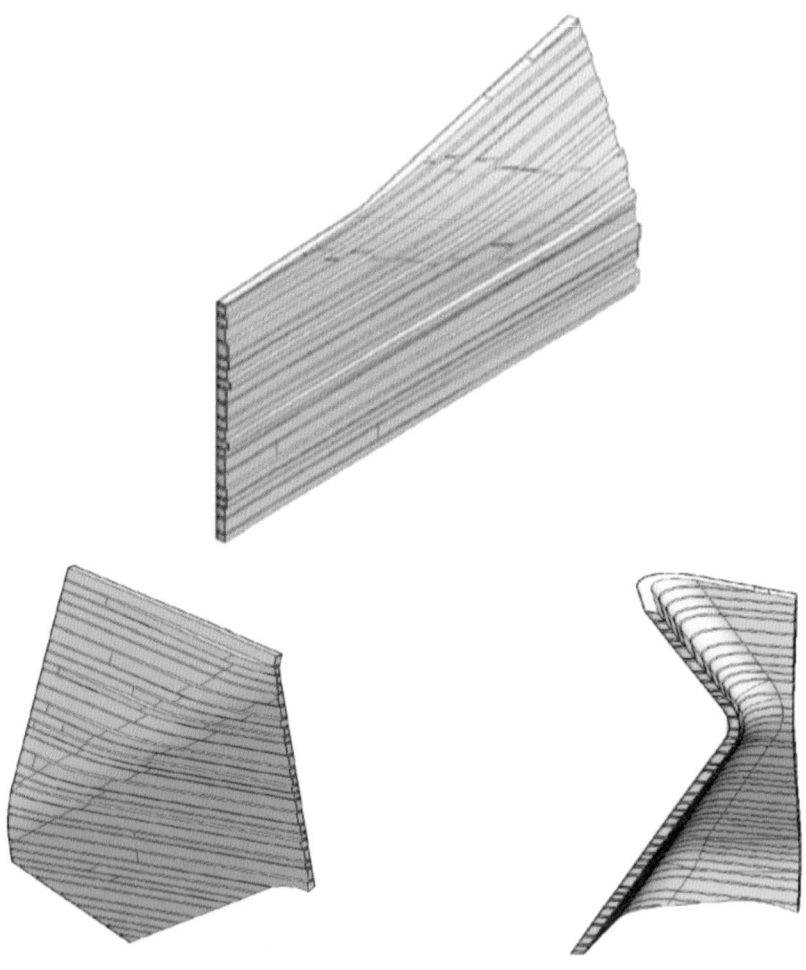

Figure 3. Facade variations that would be composed from the twisting panels.

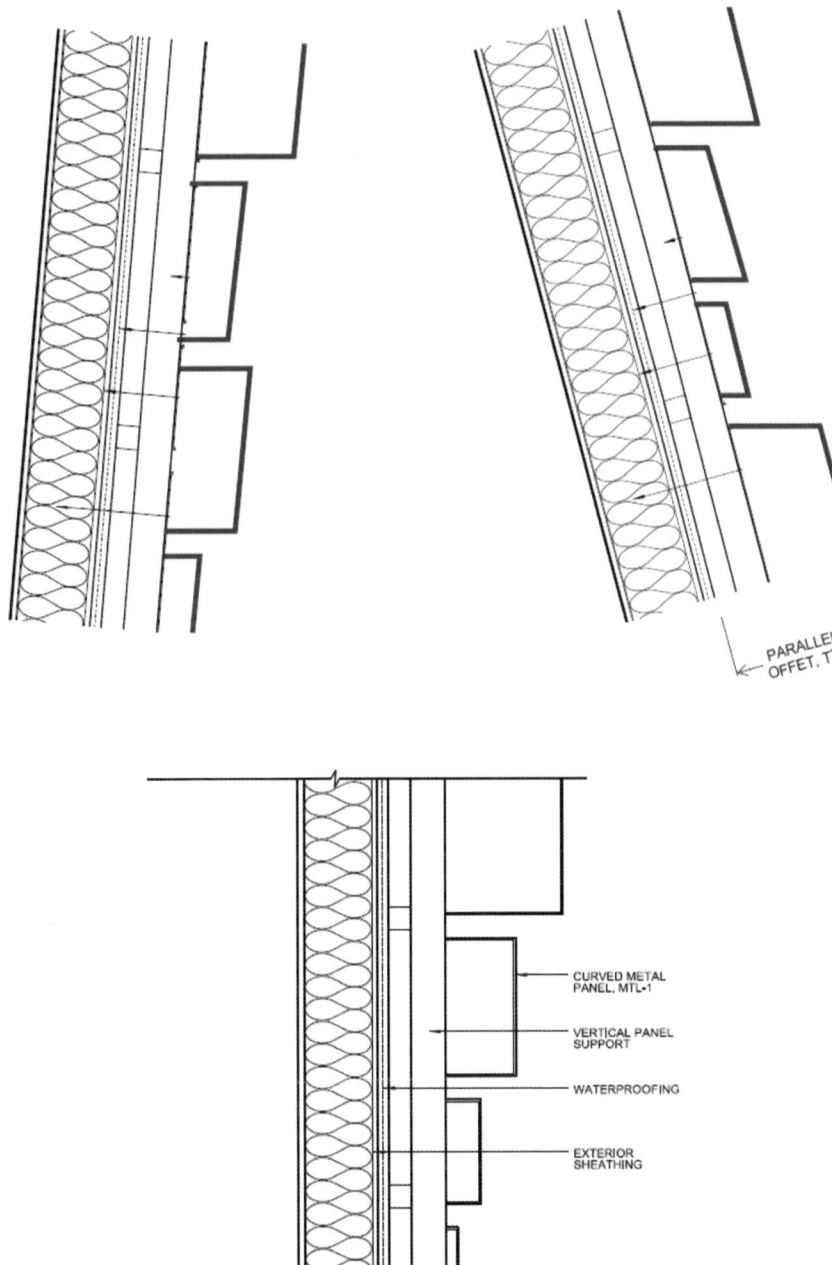

PARALLEL
OFFET, TYP

CURVED METAL
PANEL, MTL-1

VERTICAL PANEL
SUPPORT

WATERPROOFING

EXTERIOR
SHEATHING

INSULATION AND
METAL FRAMING

Figure 4. Section details of shifting conditions along the wall.

The team chose to customize a conventional extruded panel to produce their varied curved panels (Figure 5). Extrusions, an efficient way to manufacture terracotta panels, rely on uniformity to maintain structural integrity of the panel. The process requires a fixed profile through which equalized pressure of the material can be exerted, resulting in a consistent inner webbed structure and uniform panel length. However, in an extrusion that needs to curves around a surface and changes direction or curvature from positive to negative, length and inner structure will become variable. The simple geometric move creates a lot of complexity in the material and manufacturing process. To make a true ruled surface viable from this process, it is necessary to mechanically manipulate the extrude panel in three directions while also varying the length cuts and the top and bottom cuts. The curvature produces drift within the panel's internal support cells. To produce a positive to negative curvature with a single extrusion requires a tool that can post-process the panel with a speculative CNC that manipulates the clay in four dimensions as it is coming off an extrusion line.

Since that machine does not exist, the extrusions needed to be post-processed manually to achieve the desired curved forms. The team went through a series of studies with Boston Valley in the pre-workshop phase where they manipulated and stretched panels over curved forms. Bending creates micro tears in the clay body, so the assessment of tear strength became critical in gauging the ability of the material to be moved through an industrial process and reformed. To further understand the limitations of the material, during the workshop the team tried to push the curve further. Using freshly extruded slabs, they manually created bends of 20, 30, and 40 degree. Getting the slab to follow the form of a cradle alternated with trying to identify the point at which the angle of curvature would create micro tears destroying the structural integrity of the material. Defining the curvature that could be achieved without developing micro tears helped set the limits on the slope of the building facade.

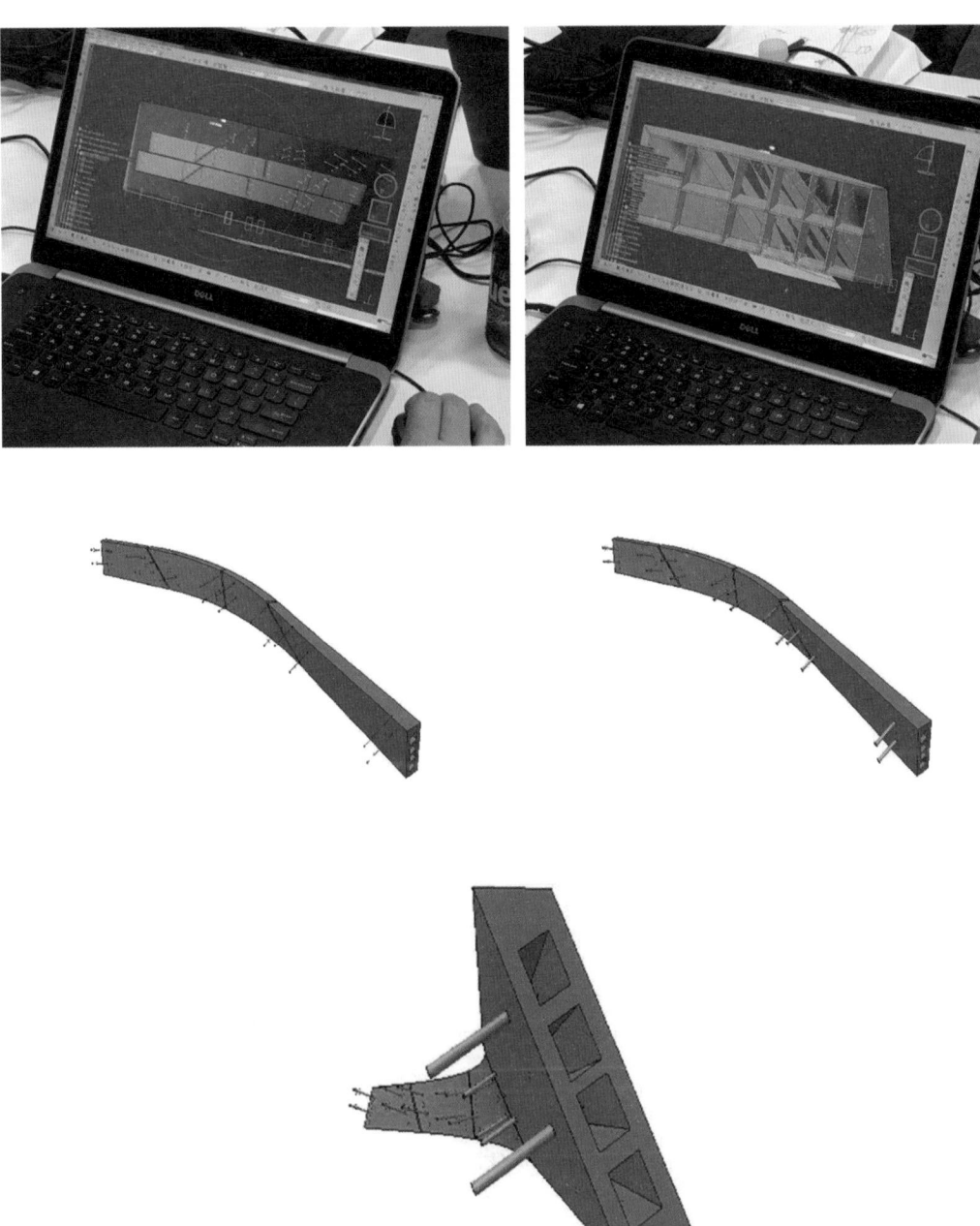

Figure 5. Prototype development involving location of the points of attachment.

During the workshop, considerable effort went into exploring the assembly system for these panels (Figures 6, 7, and 8). This involved mocking up at full scale an attachment system to connect curving panels to a curving substructure, which are not necessarily parallel to one another. A custom adjustable connector was required that worked similarly to a point fixed glass system. A pin with a washer pre-welded to a flat plate attaches to the back of the panel by being inserted into one of its four internal webbing cells.

An unexpected advantage was that the perforations in the panel body, made the internal cell structure visible so the team could survey how its drift along the curve might affect its structural integrity (Figure 7). By plotting out the drawing full scale and adhering it to the substructure, they installed three panels in under 10 minutes. Again thinking of the feedback between design and installation - this assembly process opened speculation about creating iterations that staggered the panels and stack them in different ways to obscure the pattern of the tiles.

Figure 6. Attachment system developed during the workshop.

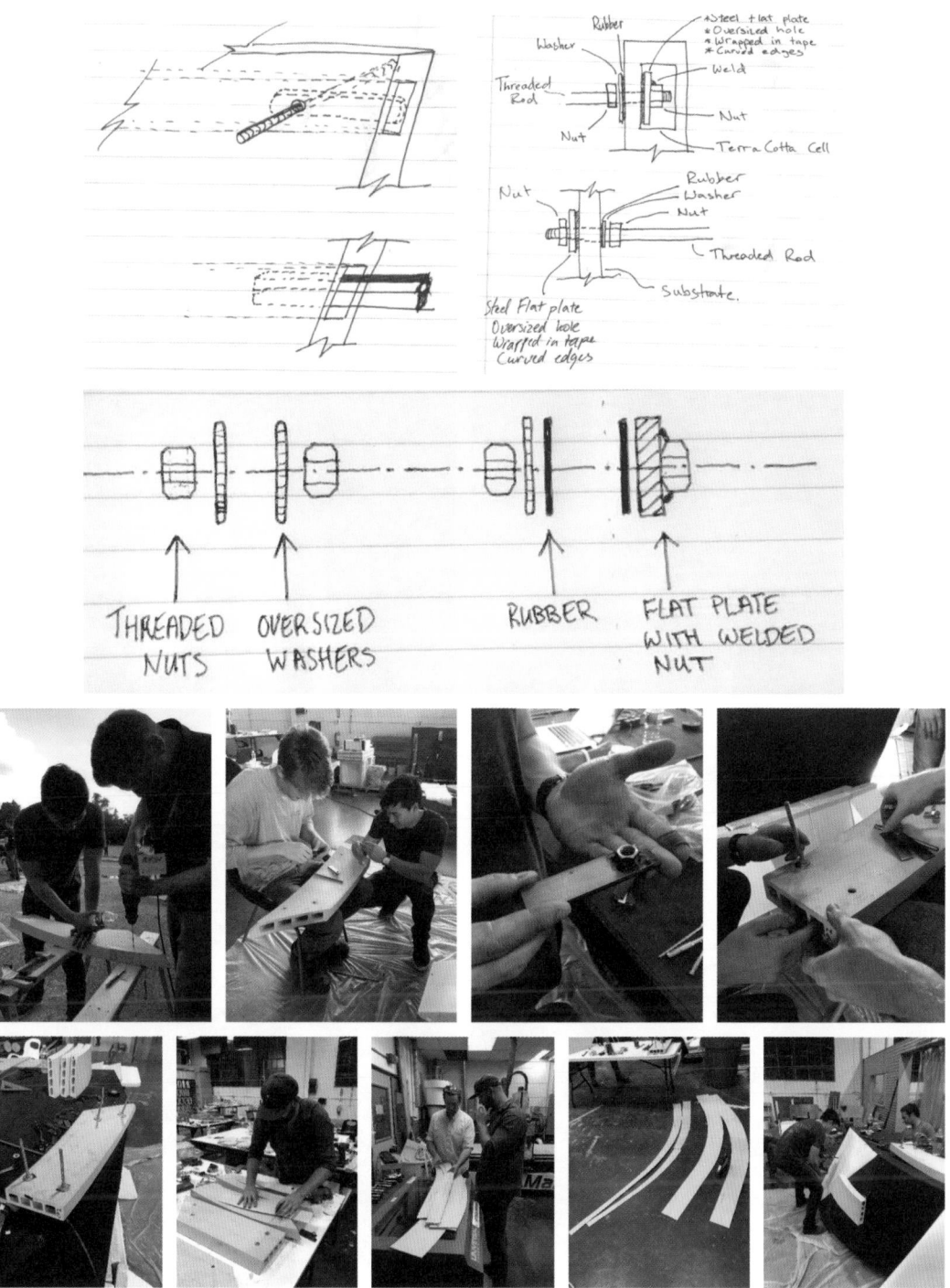

Figure 7. Design and development parallels
testing and assembly of the prototypes.

Figure 8. Parallel digital and analog processes
advance the design and assembly of the system.

The team was not only interested in taking advantage of terracotta's properties to adjust to the building form and provide self-shading, but proposed to augment the buildings environmental responsiveness due to terracotta's thermal mass, and evaporative cooling potential for a sunny, dry, breezy, site with no risk of freeze thaw. During the workshop, they tested the thermal heat gain of different colored terra cotta panels: black, white, and red. They built chambers to measure the temperature gradient on the exterior and the interior. As expected, the black panel had a higher temperature increase than the white across the exterior surface and inside the chamber. However, the red panel had an even greater increase, which was a result of a variation in the clay body chemistry rather than the color that became a significant finding (Figure 10).

These tests were paired with speculative explorations based on an assessment of solar radiation throughout the year. This assessment helped identify areas where more solar heat gain or more shading could be beneficial. The analysis lead to two proposals for the building based on the performative potential of terracotta. A solar chimney was planned between a dark slab and a glazed facade that would draw in air to create flow (Figure 11). The terracotta facade could be manipulated to create a bell chamber for the chimney effect. In another location, for a grand exterior staircase, they proposed applying waterlogged porous terracotta pavers to provide evaporative cooling (Figure 12).

Figure 9. The finished assembly in the sun
demonstrating self shading and shadow casting
on its surface.

Figure 10. The team made thermal heat gain
testing chambers to compare heat sink of different glaze and clay body choices.

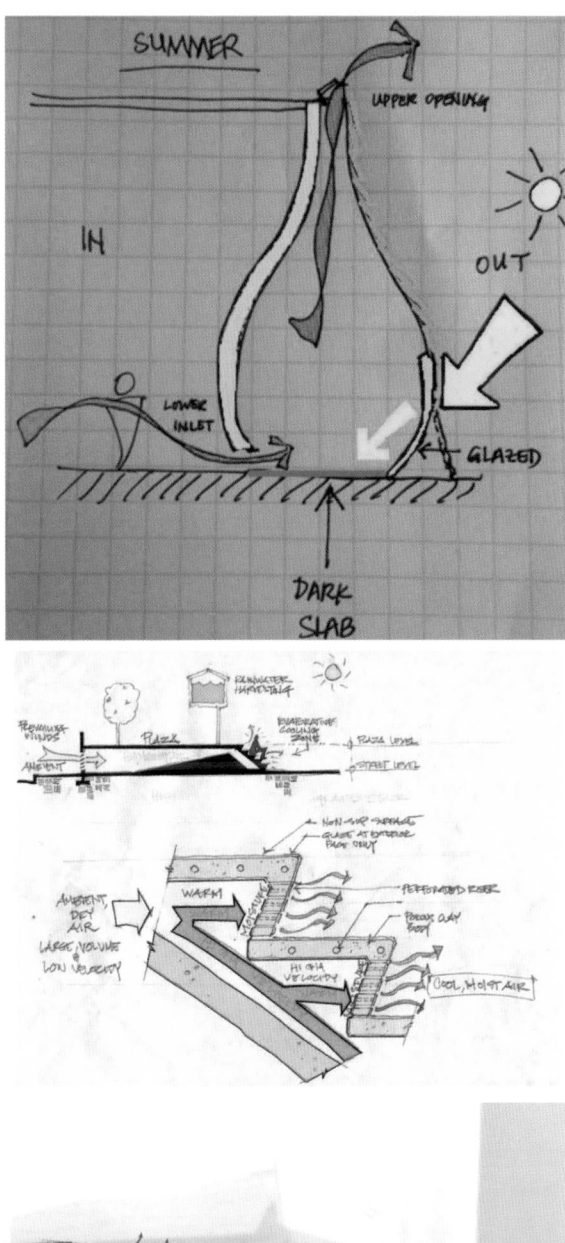

Figure 11. Solar chimney bell chamber with terracotta cladding.

Figure 12. Black, white, and red terracotta
panels being tested for drybulb temperature
gradients.

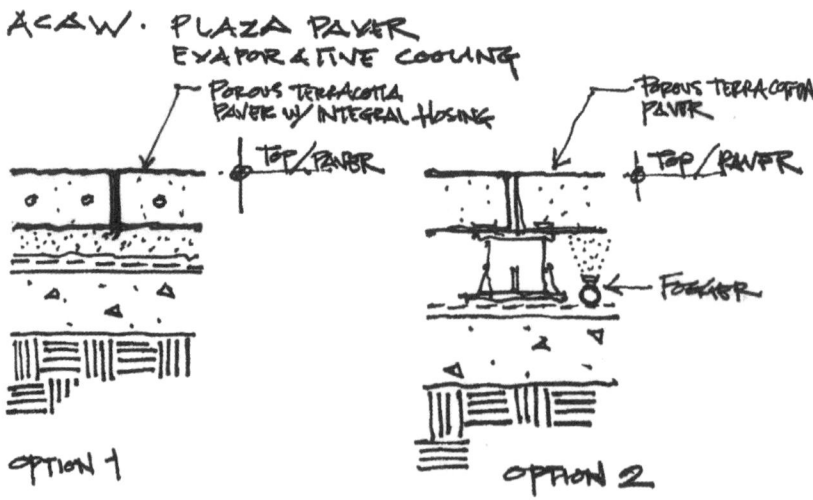

Figure 13. Terra Cotta evaporative
cooling stairway steps and plaza pavers.

Figure 14. Rendering of the proposed panels
across a facade.

Stan Su, Chris O'Hara, and Cory Brugger (left to right) plan the prototype assembly with Team Morphosis.

Performative Ornament

Team UB/Alfred

Zach Fields, Laura Garófalo (coordinator), Jason Green, Yasmiri Hiciano, Omar Khan, Grant Landreth, Casey Reas, Peter Schmidt, and John Wightman. Contributors during ACAW: Barry Grinder, Alexander Kellum, Joshua Stein, and Linda Zhang

The University at Buffalo and Alfred University team used ACAW to explore the possibilities of using ornamentation as a means to enhance bioclimatic performance. They addressed thermal absorption and buffering coupled with airflow, light and luminance for optical play, and the potential for seasonal insulation and cooling through three different design proposals; the Torus Screen, Slide Shingle and Flip Shingle (Figure 1). Since ornamentation was to be performatives they focused on surface topology and glazing techniques. These were developed through parametric pattern development, digital sculpting and CNC mold making. They also explored alternative assembly systems, like shingles and cable screens, as way to find a more flexible way to array terracotta tiles across a surface.

The three designs explored the potential of ornament as a system rather than as an object. This allowed it to work at two scales of perception. Up-close, the haptic quality of the glaze on the surface provides a tactile surface, while at a distance; the patterns play optical games across primarily flat surfaces. Recognizing that fluid forms can bring interest to large undifferentiated surfaces, the patterns can express curvilinear topographies creating the appearance of three dimensionality. The designs were primarily developed through scripts in Grasshopper and Processing.

Figure 1. Slide Shingles assembly, Flip
Shingles on the floor and Torus Screen.

The Torus Screen, developed by ceramic artist Jason Green, is a shading device that plays with light transmission on its curved surface. The unit is an oblong torus shape that modulates the sun's rays to create a glowing effect (Figure 2). Each 18" torus invites one to manipulate it by either rotating it or sliding it along the cable. This haptic engagement allows the user to change the screen's thermal and luminescent performance. During the workshop, the goal was to develop options for the cabling system and make it rotationally kinetic so that it could be more adaptive to environmental conditions. The team took engineering advice from workshop participants and Boston Valley consultants and used their Grasshopper script that allowed manipulation of the pieces in three axes to develop more efficient assembly methods and dynamic aggregations (Figure 4). In addition, the team had the opportunity to assess how light and shadow, and matte and gloss finishes affected solar gain for the pieces themselves and the surface behind them (Figure 5). With Boston Valley, the team discussed the potential for the screens to not only be shading devices when hollow but also passive solar heat collectors or evaporative cooling vessels when filled. The deployment of tmultiple tori across the cable grid can create a variety of patterns and densities depending on their location and rotation. As a lightweight unitized system, it can be arrayed on a facade independent of a building's enclosure.

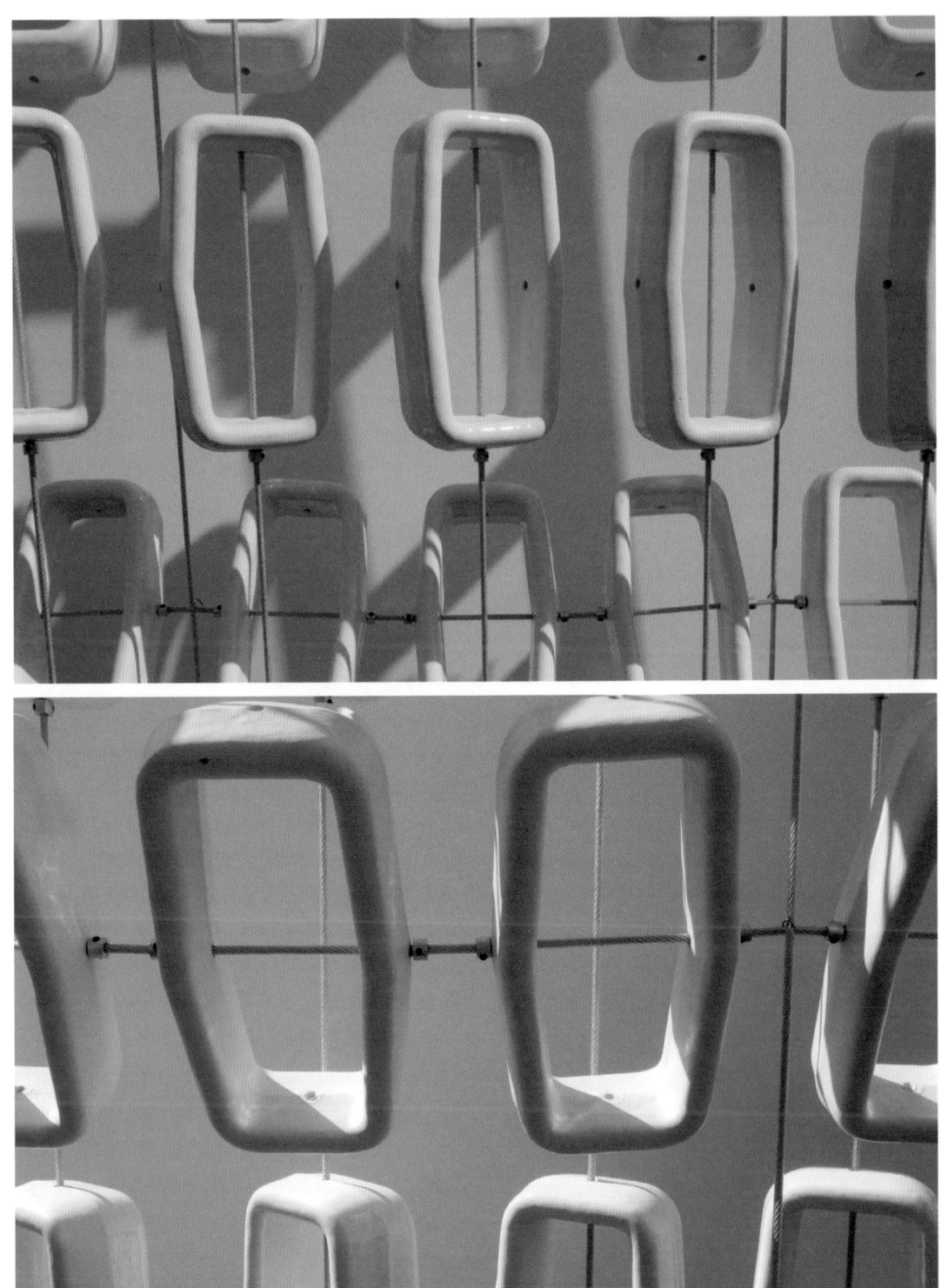

Figure 2. Torus Screen details.

Figure 3. Torus units hung in the kiln for firing to allow for glazing on all surfaces.

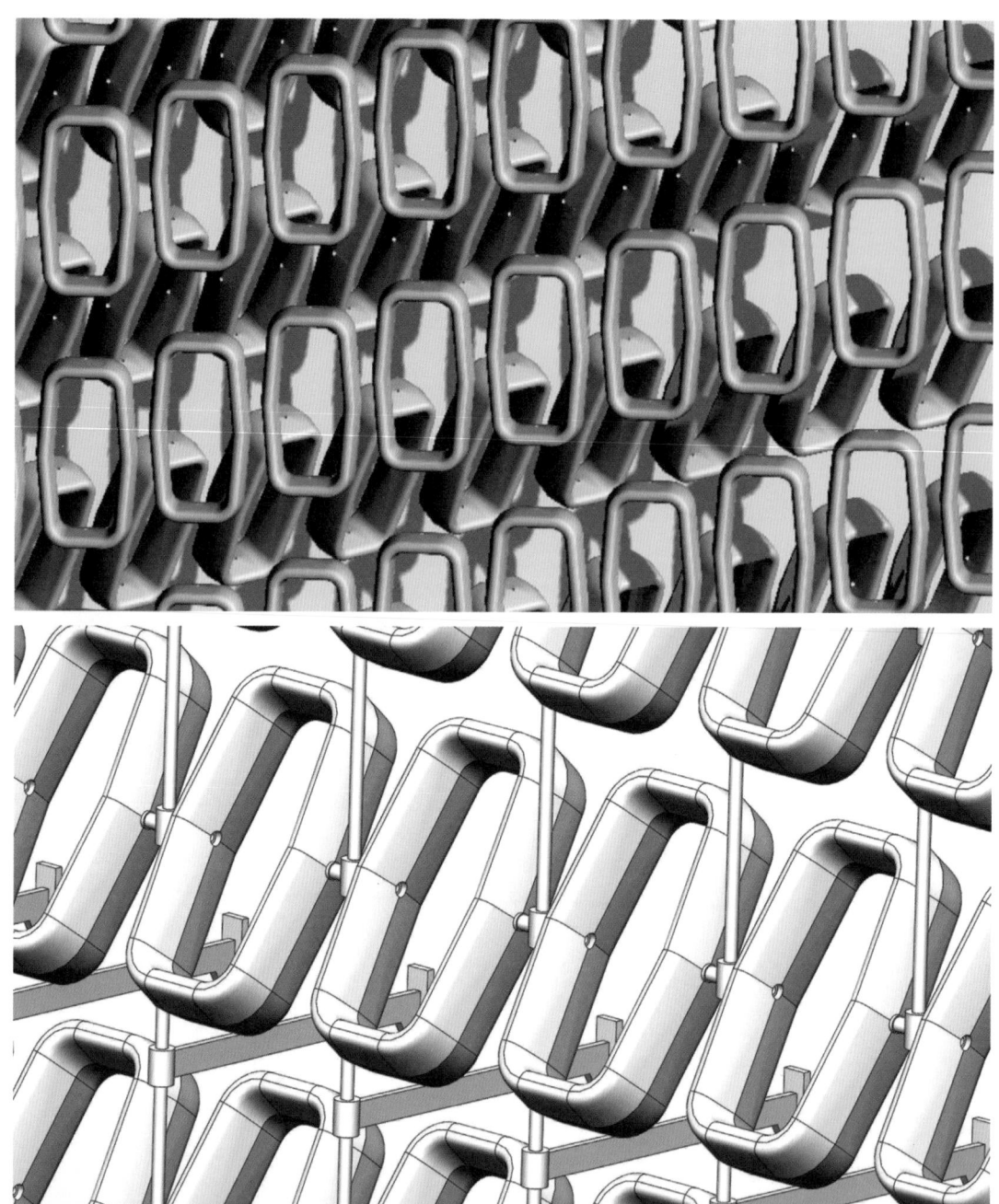

Figure 4. Detail of multiple aggregation
patterns developed in Rhino/Grasshopper.

Figure 6. Torus screen mock-up.

The team's goal with the Slide Shingle was to create a ceramic façade system that developed variation across a surface through slippage and overlap. Like a conventional wood shingle, the terracotta shingle sits over two adjacent shingles. However, because terracotta is not flexible like wood, the shingle needed to be three dimensional so that it could connect to the wall on one of its corners and slip over the adjacent tiles across the rest of its surface (Figures 6 and 7). A Grasshopper script was developed to explore shingle arrays that resulted from gradual shifting of the units based on simple linear attractors. The team found that a thirty degree line created the most fluid gradations and created ornamental effects across the surface (Figure 10). Also, glazing patterns on the tile altered not only the perception of the ornamental effect, but also its thermal performance. During the workshop, the team focused on deploying the prototype tiles and understanding the ease of their assembly. Patterns on the tiles acted as registration marks to more easily align the shingles into the desired locations (Figure 12). The overlap and registration marks work together to create visual variety even though a single tile is being repeated. As the surface tightens and or loosens thermal and air flow conditions change (Figure 8). Thermal readings of the assembly taken at the workshop showed a ten degree difference between the terracotta surface and its subsurface.

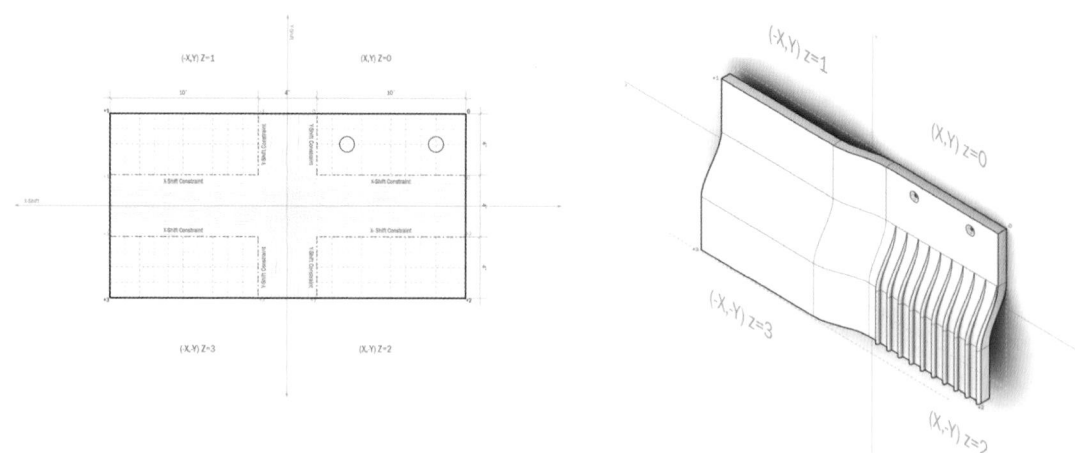

Figure 6. Slider shingle design that allows for slippage and layering of multiples to create variations while maintaining a simple attachment system.

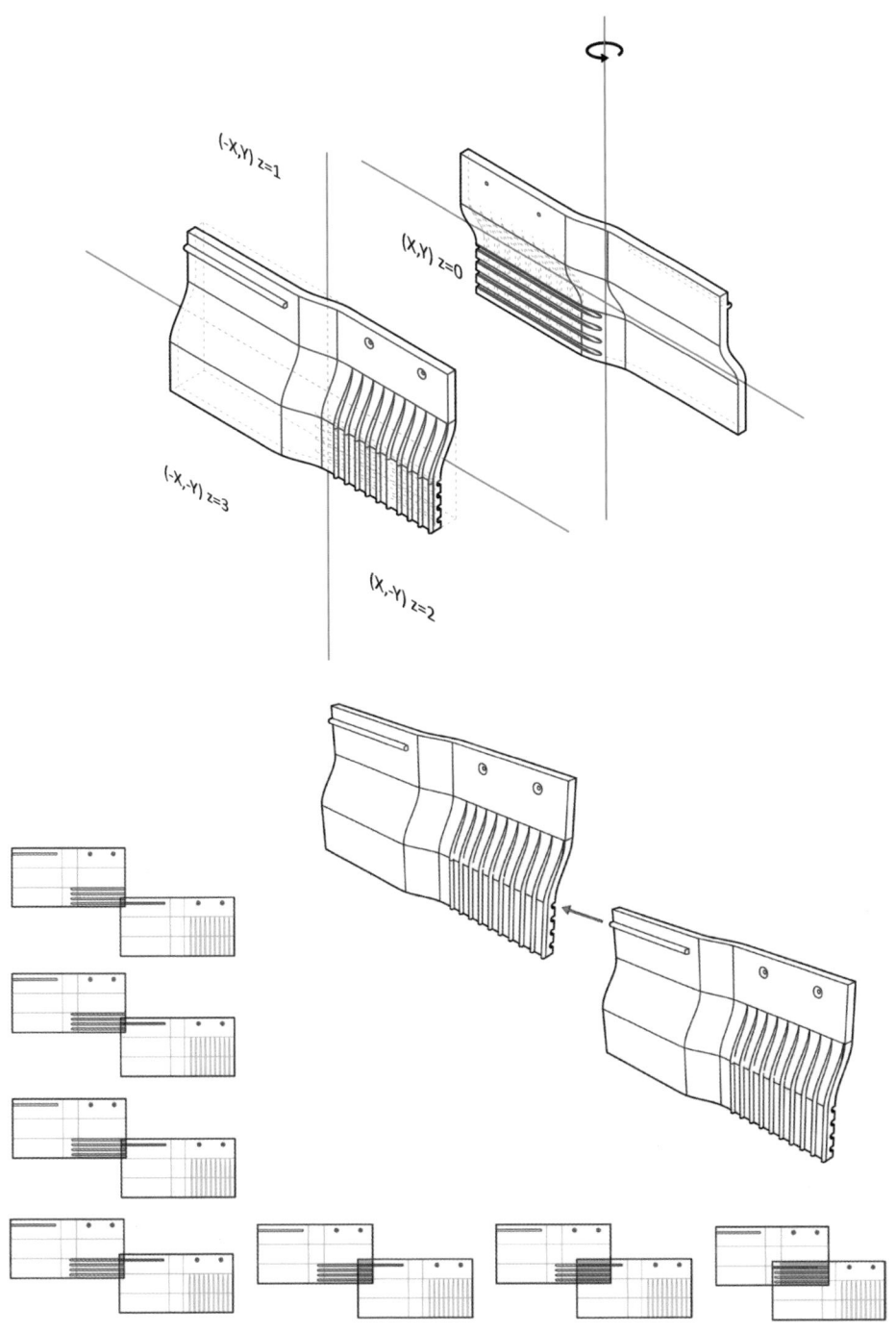

Figure 7. Registration marks become additional
surface ornamentation.

Gradient Assembly

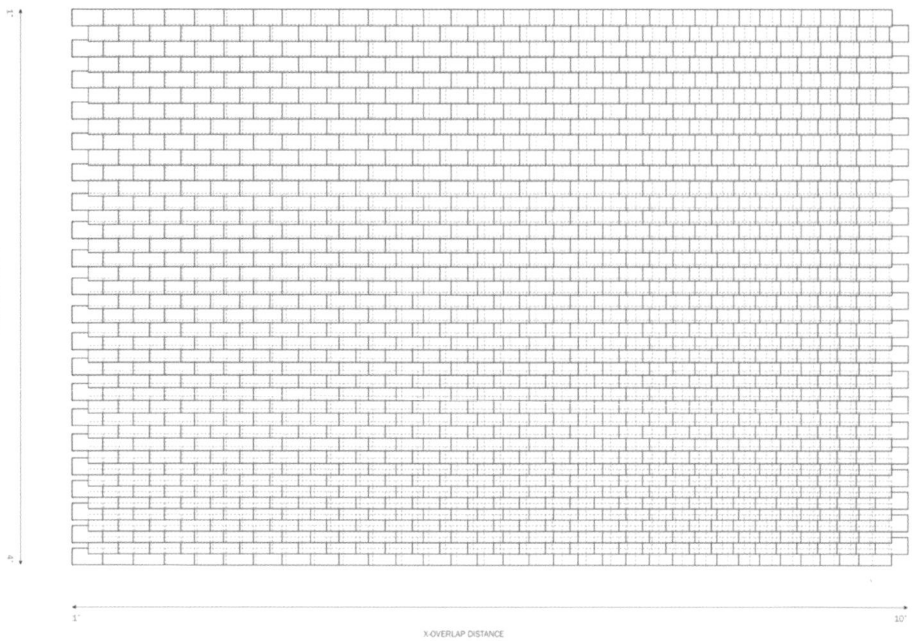

X-OVERLAP DISTANCE

1'   10'

Diagram Overlap

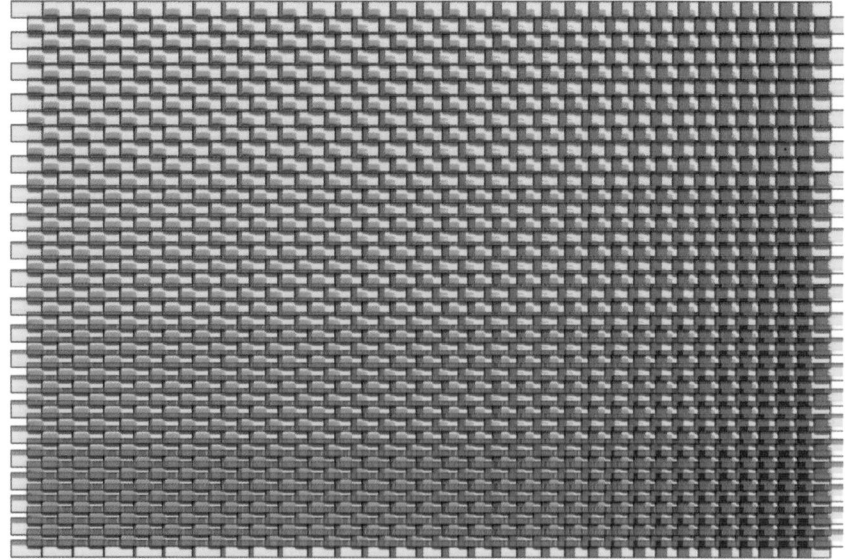

Exposed Face Diagram

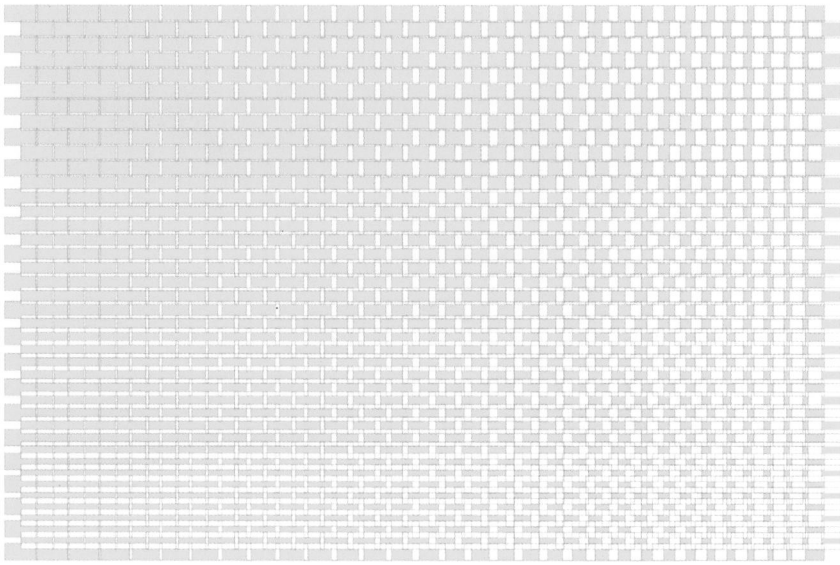

Air Opening Diagram

Figure 8. (Clockwise from top left) Diagrams
showing gradient distribution of shingles,
exposed surface for thermal absorption, openings for air circulation and a combined
performances.

Figure 9. Slide shingle assembly.

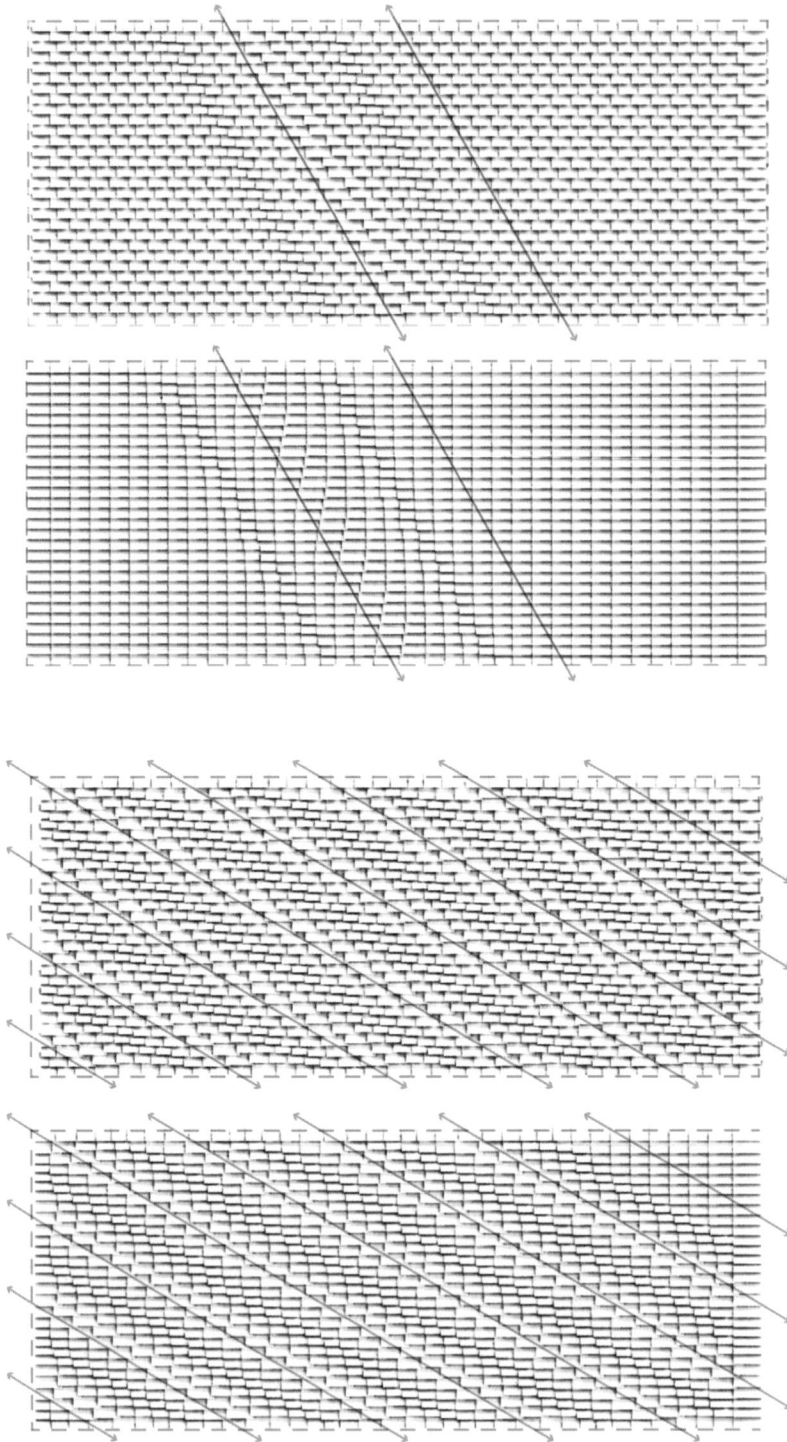

Figure 10. Parametric patterning of slide shingle surface.

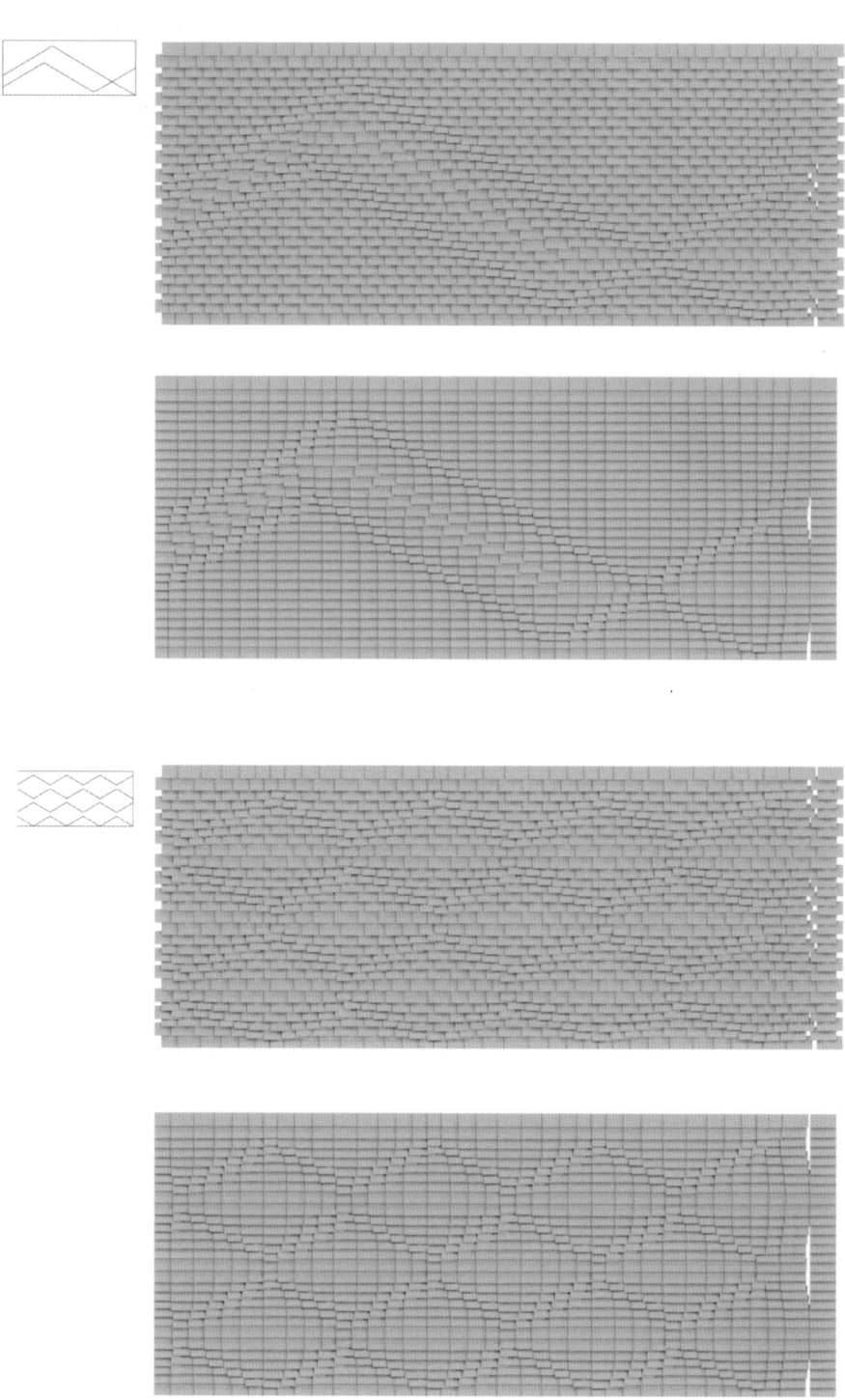

Figure 11. Parametric patterning of slide shingle surface.

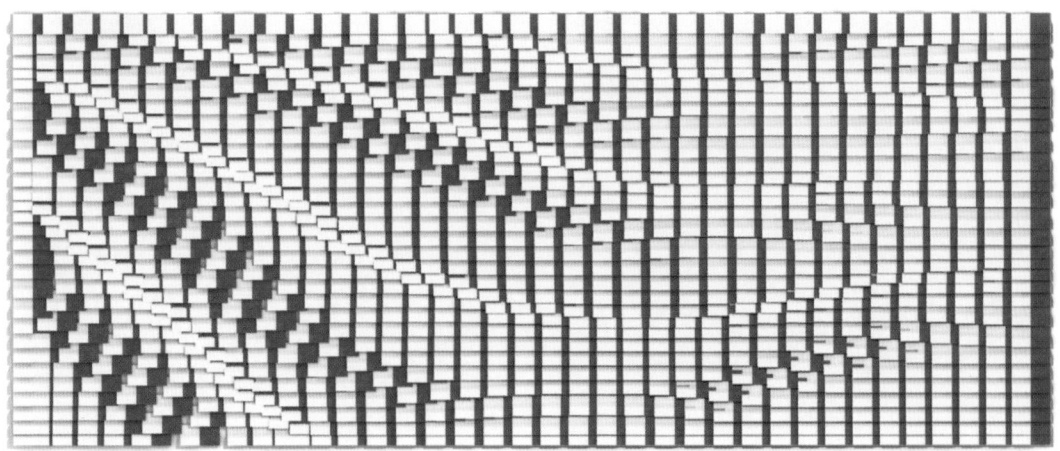

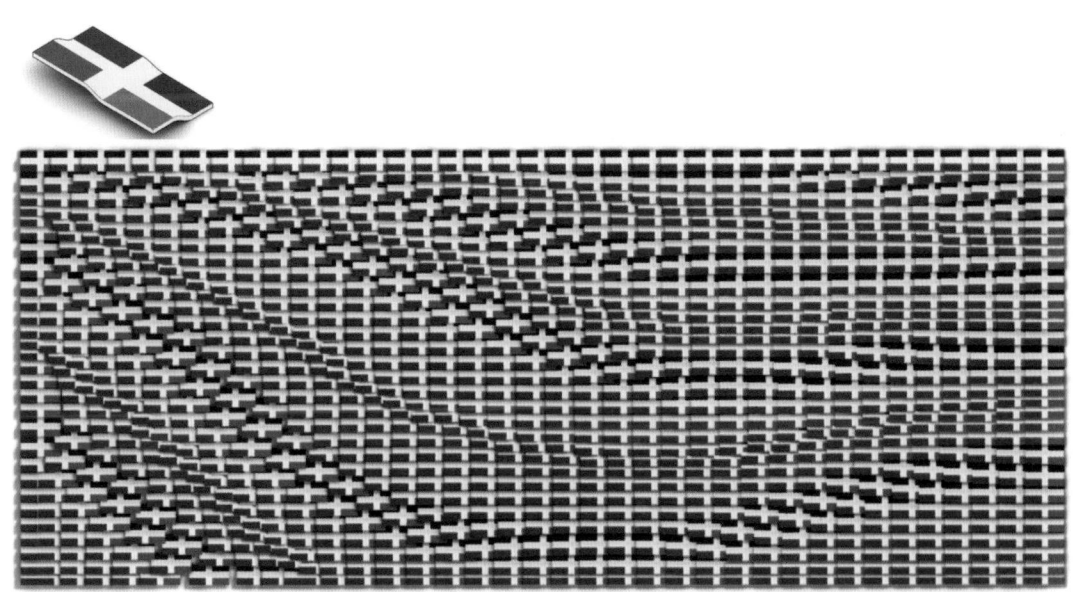

Figure 12. Patterned facade that results from
shingles colored to enhance thermal properties.

Team UB/Alfred reviewing alternative patterns generated for the Flip Tile.

Finally, the Flip Shingle gave the opportunity to use graphic production tools in thinking about ornament at the scale of the system as opposed to the object. Graphic artist Casey Reas developed a tool in Processing to help visualize the effects of changing patterns across arrayed units (Figure 14). The system gives a flat façade three-dimensional qualities just through the rotation of the unit and change of glazing pattern. The team also explored the unit topology to allow each shingle to be able to collect snow and ice so that in the winter months it could use the weather to create seasonal insulation. The resulting scalloped surface would, in the summer months, self-shade to maintain a cooler wall surface. Thermal readings taken during the workshop supported these assumptions. The topological surface variation also had visual effects that paralleled the glazing pattern simulations. The tile appeared to change color based on its orientation amplifying the undulations created by the *flip* (Figures 11, 12, and 13).

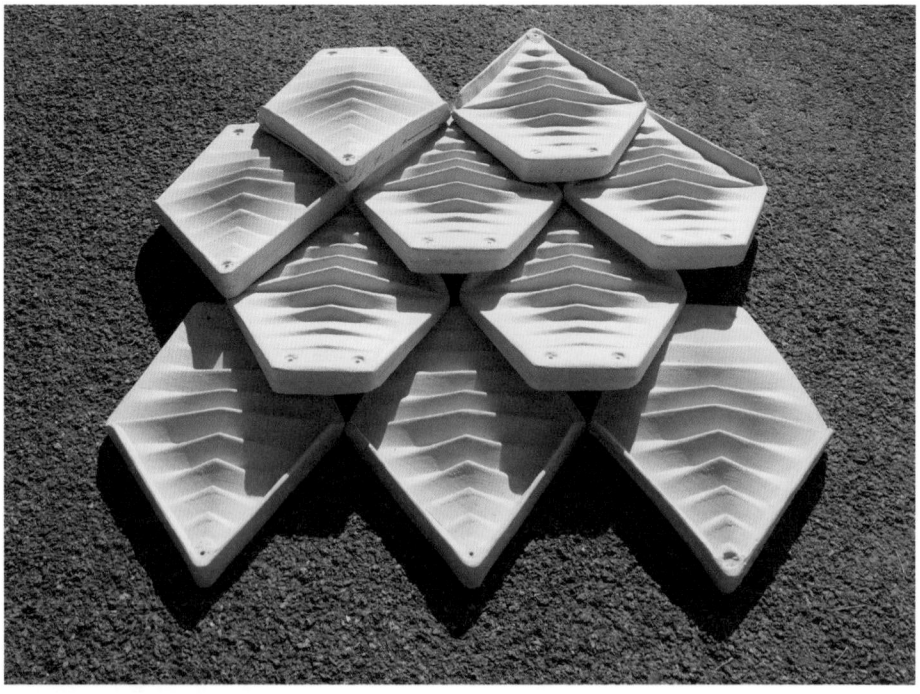

Figure 13. Flip Shingle.

Figure 14. Flip Shingle aggregation.

Figure 15. Flip Shingle creating pattern
though the re-orientation of the unit

Figure 16. Pattern variations studied through
Processing script developed by Casey Reas.

Figure 14. Pattern variations studied through Processing script
developed by Casey Reas.

HyloForm Ceramics

Team Walter P Moore

Eric Verboon (coordinator), Marty Augustyniak, Noah Burwell,
Graham Clegg, Gerd Hoenicke, Marco Juliani, Frank Kramer,
Quincy Koczka, Matt Kreidler, Matthew Stephenson

The Walter P Moore team's project approached the concept of bioclimatic design from a structural perspective. They proposed a hybrid-logic (HyLo) by introducing additional material properties to the assembly while maintaining and exploiting the inherent properties of terracotta. The design focused on a cellular structural formations that could provide environmental performance in relation to heating and cooling, insulation, thermal mass, and ventilation. The pre-workshop design phase focused on a component that creates entire structures or can be aggregated into a larger unit to create more standardized facade elements (Figure 2). The workshop week was focused on the assembly prep and installation of these components, and speculation on variations for aggregation.

Since the team was primarily composed of structural and facade engineers, the main source of inspirations came from vaulting as it couples structural and spatial perspectives. They drew inspiration from vaulting used in classical designs like those with terracotta assemblies such as the Guastavino tiling system, as well as modern applications like the work of Uruguayan architect and engineer Eladio Dieste. This was followed with research of contemporary examples that used composites to create modules that aggregate into larger spatial structures.

Based on this set of interests they explored ways to adapt the body of the terracotta ceramic mix to create a hybrid that would give additional properties to terracotta to develop a compressive structure. Initial conversations with Boston Valley team and ceramic artists about what might be possible to insert as a matrix into the clay to give it these additional properties did not yield many possibilities that would not be compromised during the firing process. Alternatively, they looked to develop a component that could pair with other materials to give it the properties they were trying to achieve.

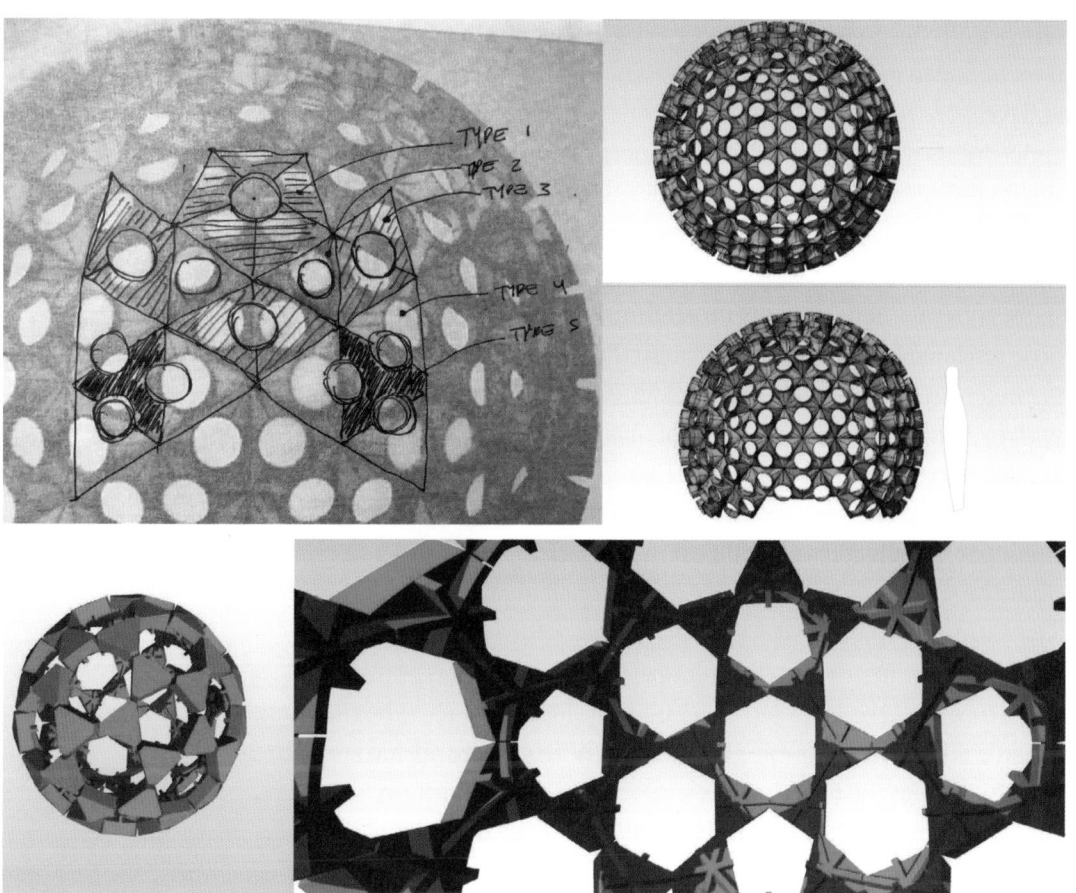

Figure 1. Pre-studies.

Historically, terracotta was used as a load bearing structural component due to its material property of being good in compression and weak in tension. More recently, it has been used in rain screen applications where its structural properties are not utilized. These screens hang on metal cables, rods or tracks. The team speculated on bringing the two materials together to create a structural composite through post-tensioning. In traditional post tensioning of concrete slabs, you get efficiency from much thinner concrete slabs by adding post-tensioned steel tendons through them. In this case, post tensioning provided compression back into the components in keeping with examples of post tensioning of masonry enclosures rather than as a primary structural condition. Examples are found in restoration where reinforcement of a masonry facade is concerned and post-tensioning is introduced to stabilize it.

The team conceived of tiles with post-tensioning tendons running through them, arrayed in different patterns within a larger unitized panel that could be installed on a building (Figures 5–10). The tile module is highly repeatable and provides both structural and spatial conditions that the team was seeking. They took inspiration from the Fish-Eye dome by Buckminster Fuller. The tile is a triangle with a subtle convex surface that can array into pentagons and hexagons (Figure 1). These can tile a polyhedra that would be equivalent to a thin shell. Instead of it being purely in compression, the shell would be in tension as well.

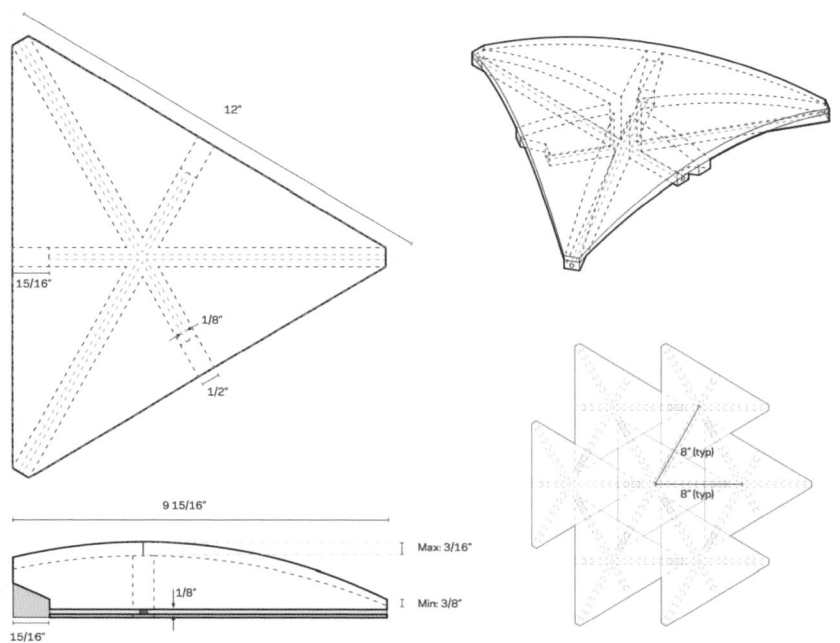

Figure 2. The unit and its aggregation.

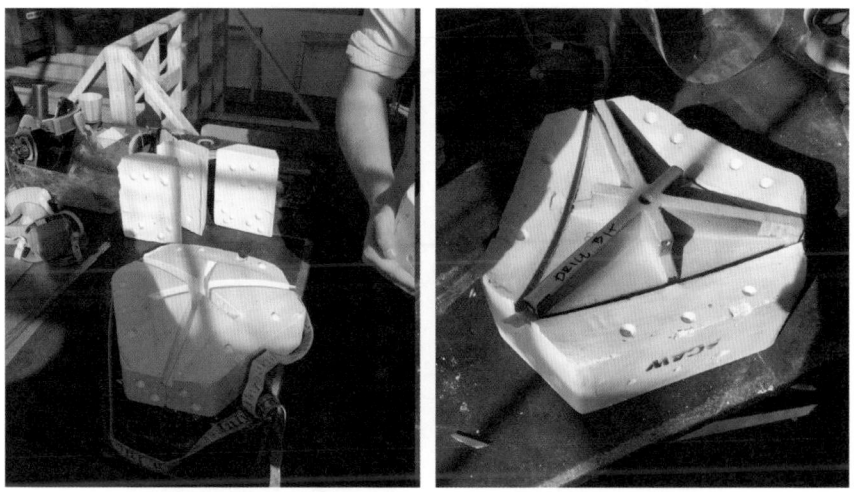

Figure 3. Unit in its plaster mold.

The assembly of the tiles took the majority of the workshop week (Figure 4). The module interlocks in a three-way grid through which tension and compression cables run (Figure 11). The units were slip-cast with holes for cables to run through the webbing, but working the cables through post firing proved to be challenging. However, through brainstorming and working together they were able to solve the assembly and manufacturing problems. Some unique solutions needed to be developed like cutting up raw rubber boots to create isolator gaskets that could be placed between the tiles to prevent chipping the beautiful glaze. Real knowledge was gained from the hands on engagement with the fired terra cotta modules regarding the ease of install. The second assembly went together in about an hour while the first one took a better part of a few days (Figure 7). The team also explored other options for the unitization by using CNC'd tiles out of wood with the help of the University at Buffalo students on the team (Figures 7 and 8). This opened explorations about how the structure supports itself and how the surfaces can be treated.

Figure 4. Inventive assembly techniques and materials.

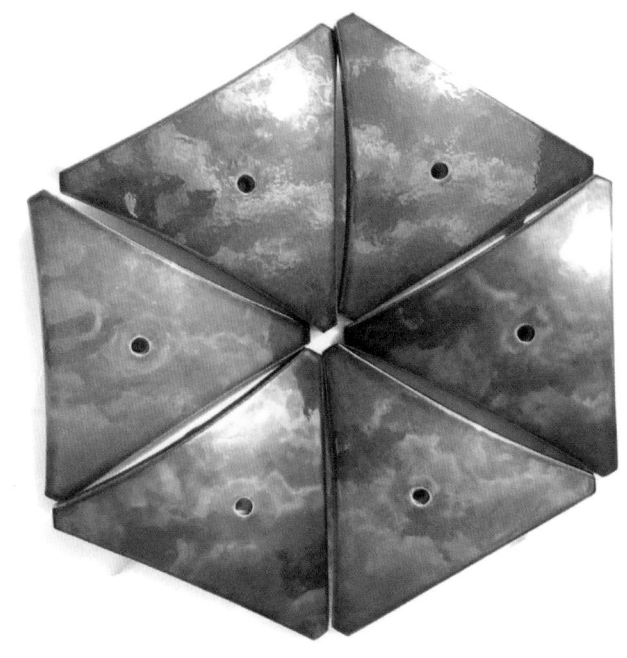

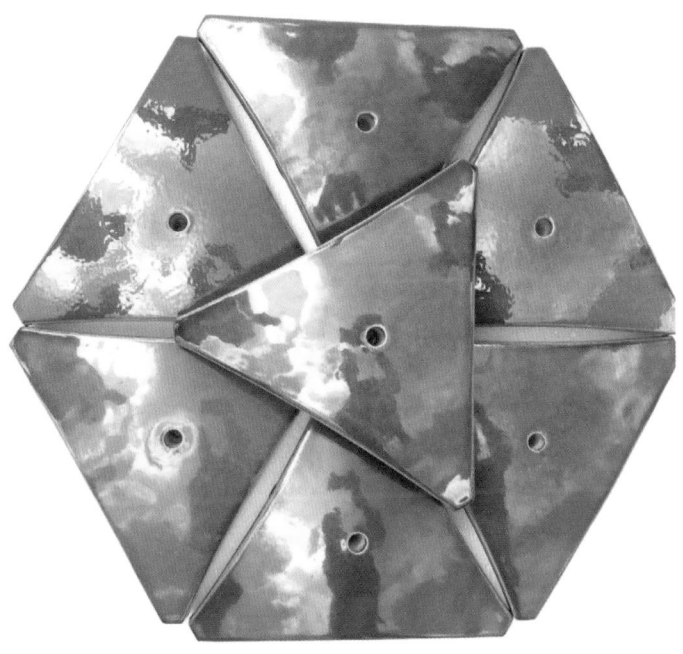

Figure 5. Variations in assembly patterns.

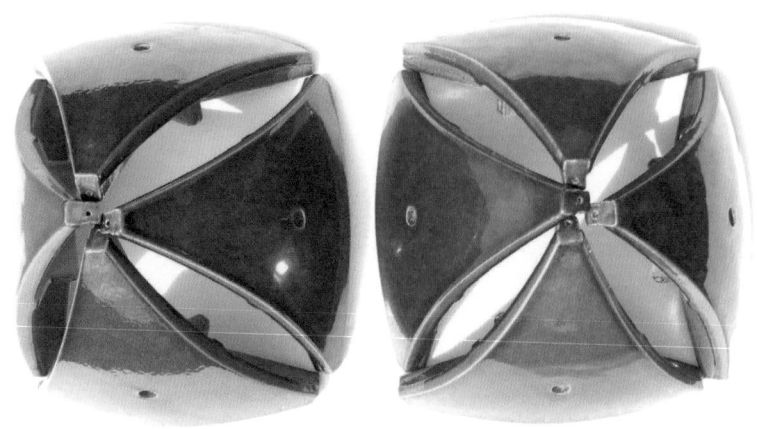

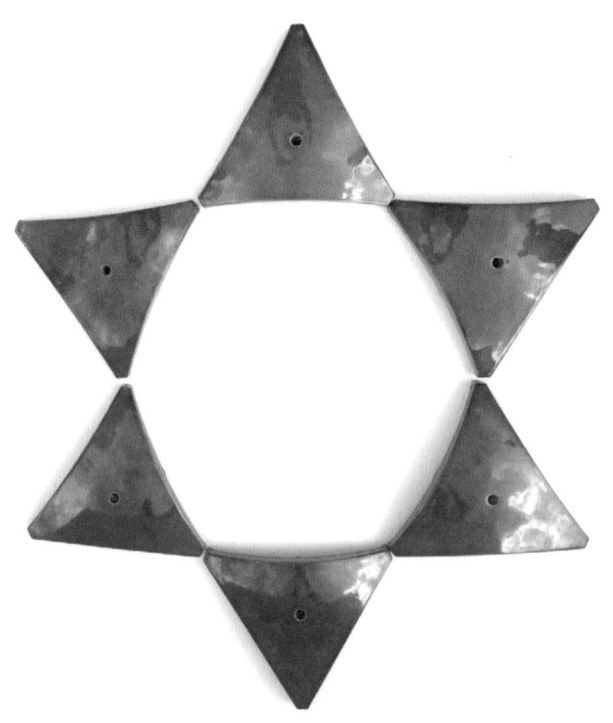

Figure 6. Variations in assembly patterns.

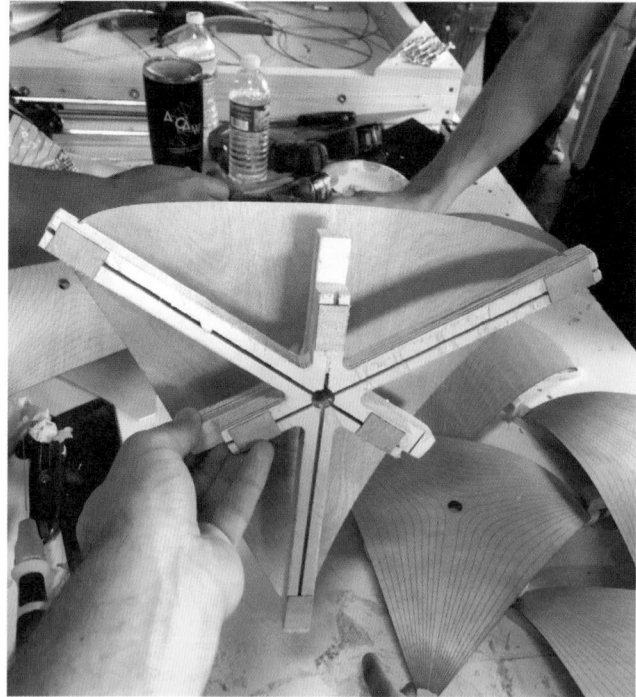

Figure 7. Wood prototype assembly.

Figure 8. Laser scored details on wood
prototypes.

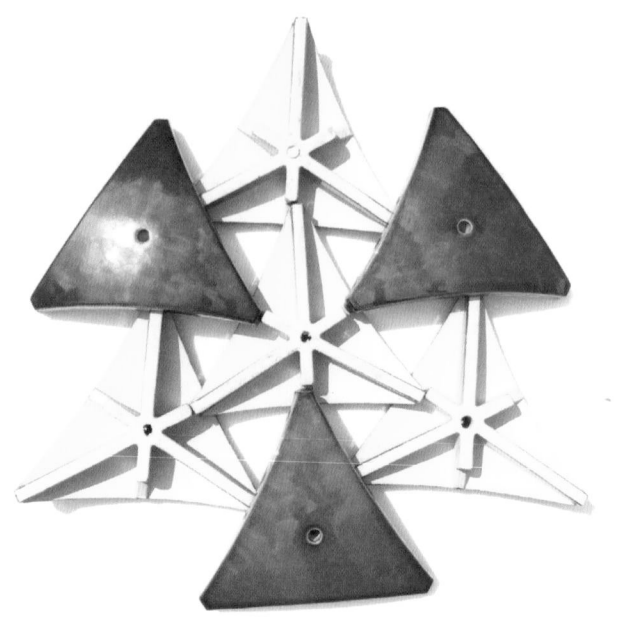

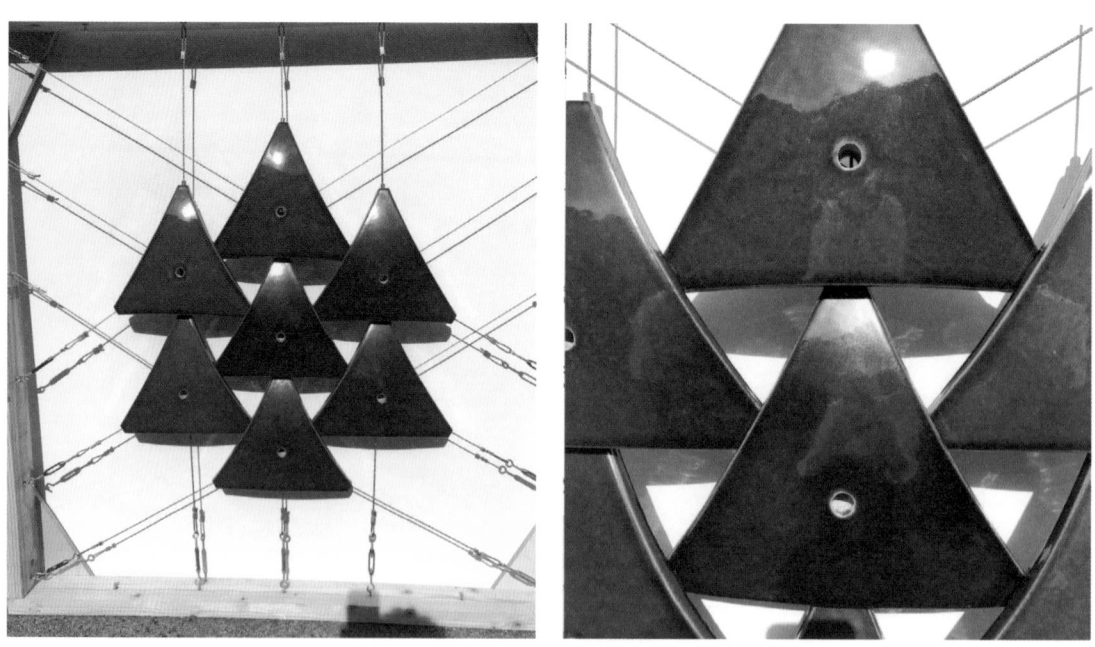

Figure 9. Final unitized assembly.

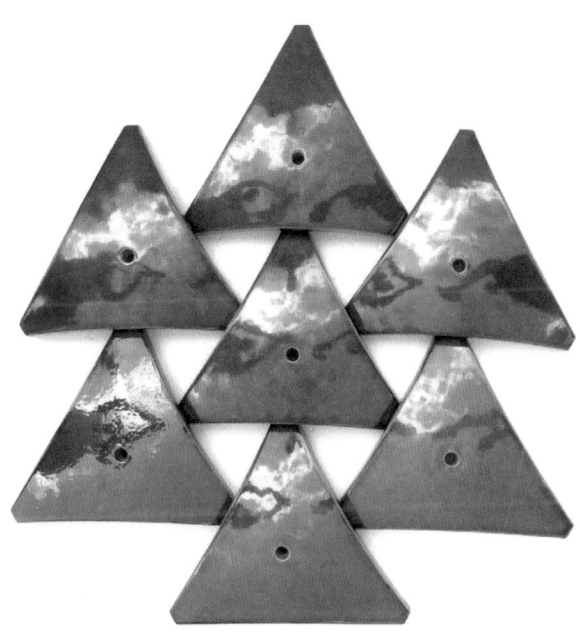

Figure 10. Front and back view of the assembly tiles.

Figure 11. Assembly design.

Figure 12. Threading the tiles.

The prototyping was coupled with digital modeling exploring how to populate the tile module across different surfaces or the same surface in different ways (Figure 14–16). They explored how to unitize it in different ways so that you have hangable curving panels or slabs (Figure 13). Flipping the module so such that the shell is facing inwards and outwards to provides more opportunities for aggregation. Finally, to redesign the module itself so that it accommodates different degrees of curvature since at the moment it's limited on how far it can turn on the surface or how it can accommodate fenestration. Possible applications areas are lightweight, thin-shelled structure and screens. In certain instances, you wouldn't need an actual shell, so it would be an open rain screen to be used for shading, for example, along a western exposure.

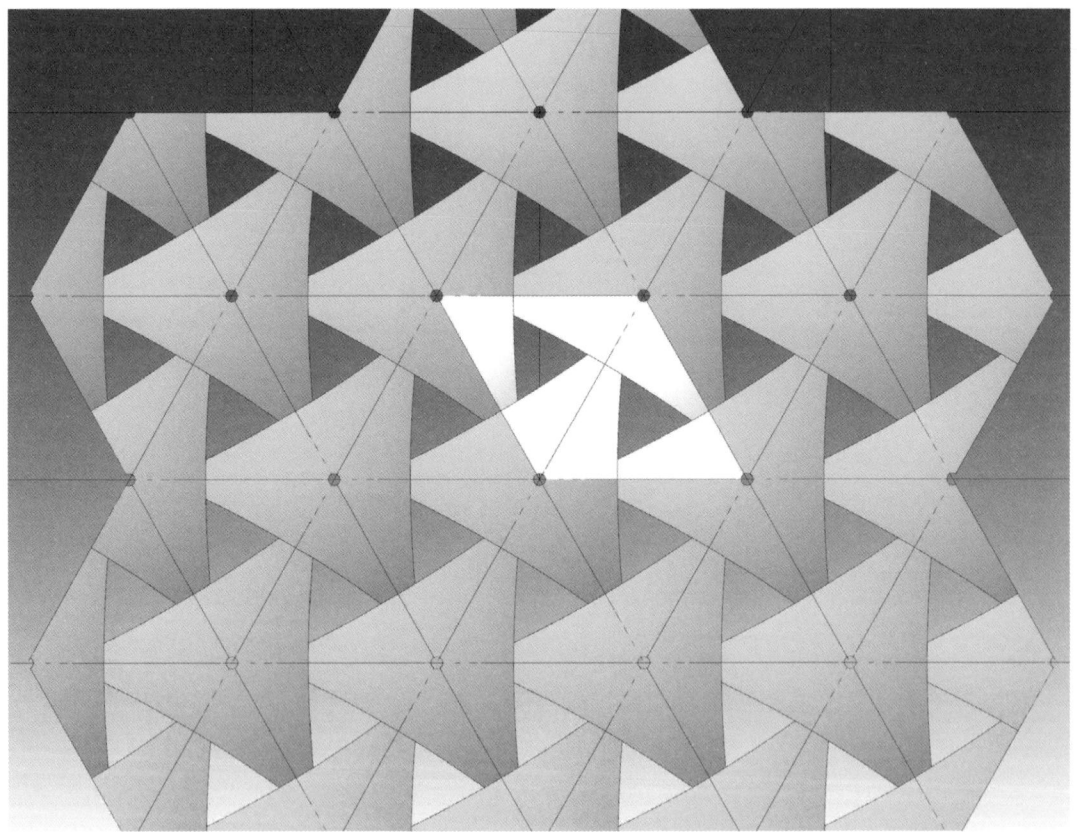

Figure 13. A more elaborate unitized panel.

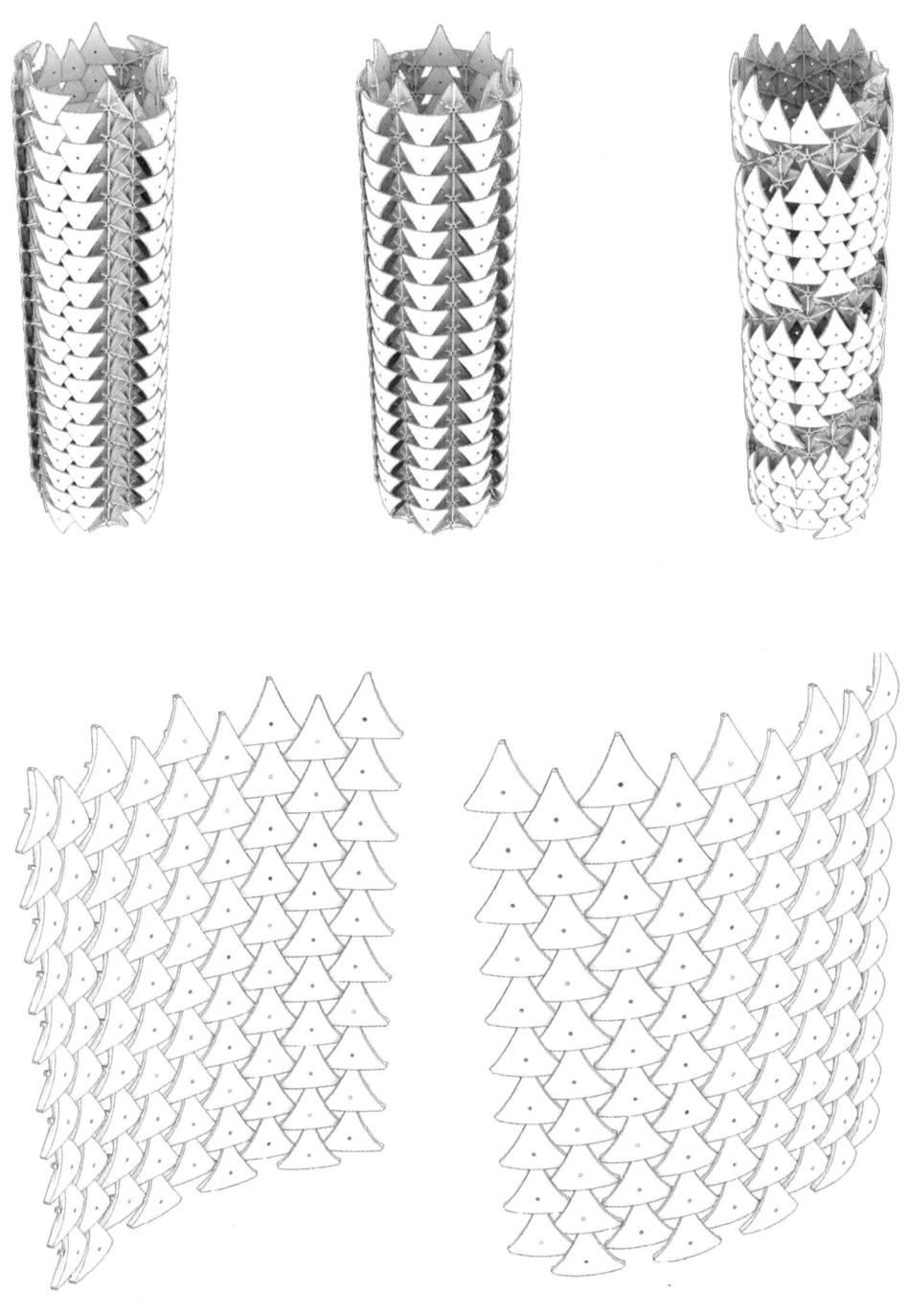

Figure 14. The module arrayed in different patterns across curved surfaces.

Figure 15. The module applied to a flat surface.

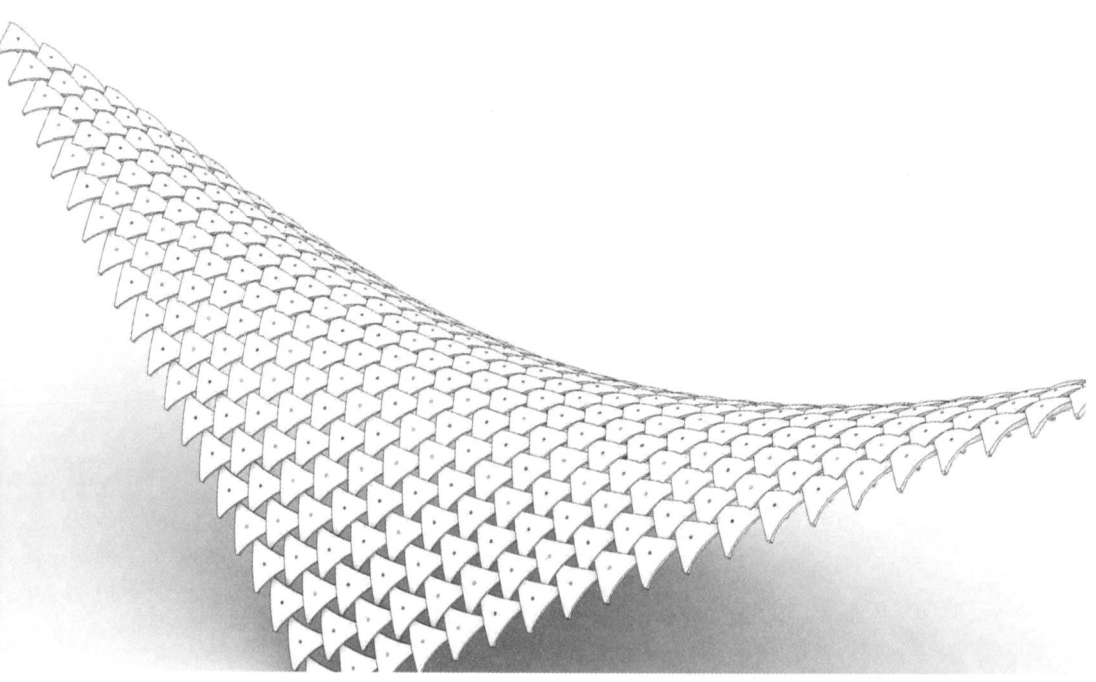

Figure 16. The module arrayed over a hyperbolic surface.

Marty Augustyniak leading a discussion on the Holyform Ceramic components for Team Walter P Moore.

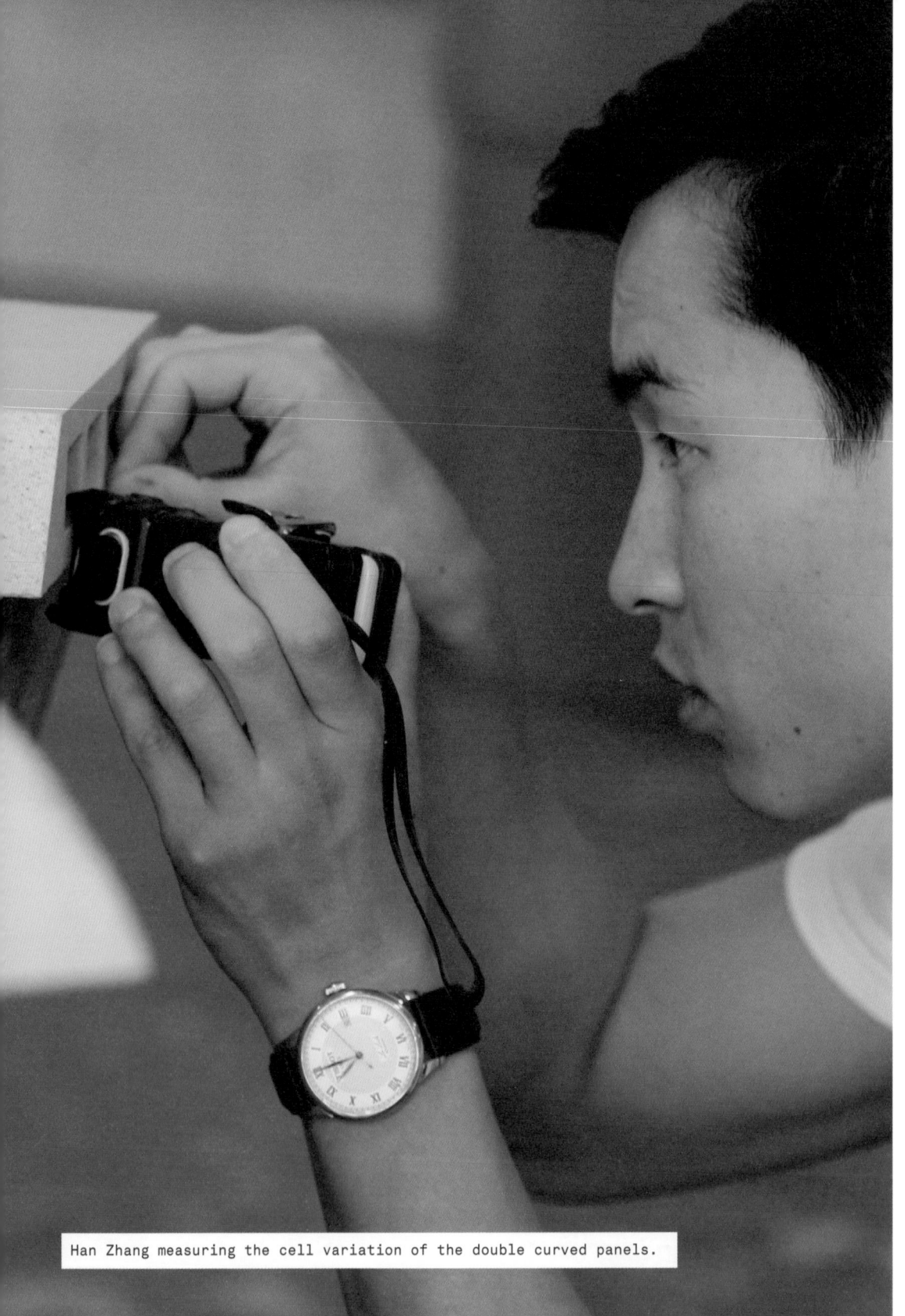

Han Zhang measuring the cell variation of the double curved panels.

Team Walter P Moore test configurations for their unitized system.

Team UB/Alfred preparing to experiment with the potterbot, a digitally controlled ceramic extruder.

Hands on assembly of the mock ups was coupled with on the fly changes based on variations in alignment.

Team Morphosis sketched alternative thermally active surface conditions for their twisted panel system.

In Dialog: Applied Research in Industry

Omar Khan
with
Dr. Krishna Rajan

The following interview with Krishna Rajan, Erich Bloch Chair and Empire Innovation Professor in the Department of Material Design and Innovation, University at Buffalo, probes what design means to material scientists. It also explores areas where material science can have more profound influence over the design of the built environment.

Omar Khan: Your department at the University at Buffalo is called the Department of Material Design and Innovation. For a materials scientist what does design mean?

Krishna Rajan: Materials science offers many analogies that can be ascribed to architectural design principles. For example the concept of "molecular architecture" is a very well established paradigm in material science. It addresses how the arrangement of "building blocks" in materials science, right from the molecular scale can define the properties of materials. Here the interface between materials and architecture is the geometrical aspect of design. It's not an accident to say that you need to have a hexagon as your most stable structure. Nature demonstrates that whether it's a snowflake or a honeycomb. So the question here is when we talk about designing materials one can design at the molecular scale or work at the micron or large scale. Hence the term design in the field of materials science and engineering captures is in fact a multidimensional term that covers many length scales and many features. Some features as we noted are geometric in nature (crystallography is a good example) while other features relate to how materials are synthesized, processed and assembled.

Materials scientists can for instance design at the molecular scale that can help direct the design at the macro scale or change the design at a higher length scale. This is a classical materials science challenge and the field of architecture provides an excellent metaphorical paradigm. However to put that architectural analogy into practice in developing materials is complex. So the name of my department, Material Design and Innovation, is a good one because it challenges the metaphorical thinking and provokes us

Hand-sculpted terra cotta ornamentation executed at Boston Valley.

as scientists on how do we actually link "design" to "innovation". We can create innovations and then work backwards and say there's a design concept that drives it or we can design something and we can then suggest where it could have impact on innovation, but it's very hard to have a seamless relationship between the two. I think the "and" is actually the gap that we're trying to fill in our department.

Khan: One of the important issues at this year's ACAW was to include prototyping as part of the design thinking process? You had in your presentation to the participants used the cooking analogy when describing making materials. Can you expand on that because I think it speaks to some of the ways in which design as process and design as product can come together?

Rajan: The cooking recipe analogy is helpful to explain what materials science and engineering is. A recipe involves both ingredients and how you cook with them. The design of materials involves not only taking into account the recipe's ingredients (e.g. chemistry) but how we process with those ingredients. A challenging question I faced when I came to talk to your workshop was trying to understand where as a material scientist could meaningfully contribute to the architectural community? And paradoxically enough, the one area that I found the closest connection to was that part of your community that was doing art. They were creating sculptures and models using various techniques, types of materials and ironically enough what would be viewed as art actually has what we're trying to do in the science.

Khan: Can you propose areas of engagement between architecture and material science that we can build on from the workshop?

Rajan: The easiest place of interaction is if we could use architecture and architectural principles to teach material science. We could also explore ways to make architects more aware of the choices you have. For instance we can interface with the architectural design community on the multitude of ways we can engineer materials that enhance the functionality at the architectural level. In this manner we can introduce the concept of "design-with-intent" where architects can help to inspire new concepts in materials science. Topics that come to mind include the development of the use of renewable materials, renewable energy to develop resilient infrastructure. This could serve as a paradigm shift where we may be able to close the gap between "design" and "innovation" we talked about earlier. Another opportunity for the intersection of material science and architecture should be the role of materials science on impacting urban planning, transportation and how that in turn could influence architectural design.

Traditional sculpting techniques utilized in restoration work at Boston Valley.

Extruded terra cotta through a square die for more contemporary design applications at Boston Valley.

Historic ornament being color matched with Boston Valley produced
clay body that will be used for the restoration.

Glaze experiments at Boston Valley that demonstrate the versatility of terra cotta and its ability to mimic other materials like stone.

Biographies

Organizers

Omar Khan is Department Chair and Associate Professor in the Department of Architecture, and co-leader in the Sustainable Manufacturing and Advanced Robotic Technologies Community of Excellence (SMART) at the University at Buffalo (SUNY). He is co-founder of the design firm Liminal Projects. He has received grants from the Rockefeller Foundation, New York State Council for the Arts and the New York Foundation for the Arts. He is widely published and is co-editor of the Situated Technologies Pamphlet Series, published by the Architectural League of New York.

John B. Krouse, President and CEO of Boston Valley Terra Cotta, holds his B.S. in Ceramic Engineering and minor in Ceramic Sculpture from Alfred University. His engineering, artistic expertise, and 32 years of experience help guide Boston Valley's manufacturing of terra cotta products for several markets while consistently expanding the state of the art facility and equipment.

Bill Pottle is Director of Business Development for Boston Valley Terra Cotta and has been with the company since 2012. The majority of his career has been spent in architectural sales working with architects and construction professionals across the globe. Bill's responsibilities include new business development, managing Boston Valley's sales network, directing marketing programs, and major contract negotiations, and managing Boston Valley's estimating and project management teams.

Speakers

Mic Patterson has made a career, study and practice of building facades. He is Director of Strategic Development for Schüco-USA, the Ambassador of Innovation & Collaboration for the Façade Tectonics Institute, and PhD candidate at the University of Southern California. He has taught, written and lectured on varied aspects of advanced façade technology, and is the author of *Structural Glass Facades and Enclosures*, a comprehensive guide to structural glass facades for architects, engineers, and builders. Mic presented the Keynote Address at the workshop titled: *Material Matters: Durability, obsolescence, adaptability and the embodied impacts of the building shell.*

Gerd Hoenicke is Director Consulting International Projects and Pre Construction Services at Schüco International KG. He gave a lecture titled "Façade Systems with terra cotta" at the workshop.

Craig Mutter, is Design Principal at CannonDesign. His projects have earned numerous design awards, and each is characterized by a skilled approach to materiality and a thoughtful approach to place Prior to joining CannonDesign, Craig led the design of the Wall-Apelt Center for Asian Art at the Ringling Museum of Art as a Principal at Machado Silvetti. Craig is a licensed architect and a LEED-accredited professional.

Dr. William Carty is the John F. McMahon Professor and Chair of Ceramic Engineering at Alfred University. He teaches extensively (engineering classes during the school year and "Ceramic Science for the Artist" workshops in the summer) and has researched all aspects of traditional ceramics production. He is a frequent contributor to NCECA.

Dr. Krishna Rajan is Erich Bloch Chair and Empire Innovation Professor in the Department of Materials Design and Innovation, School of Engineering and Applied Sciences, University at Buffalo. He is a member of the Science and Technology Experts Group: National Academies of Sciences, Engineering, and Medicine, winner of the Alexander von Humboldt Research Award and CSIRO Distinguished Visiting Scientist Fellowship, founding editor-in-chief of the *Materials Discovery Journal*, and member of the National Academy of Sciences.

Anne Currier is a ceramic artist and professor emerita at Alfred University. She has received awards from the National Endowment for the Arts, the New York Foundation for the Arts, the Virginia Groot Foundation, the Burchfield Penney Art Center, and the American Crafts Council. Her sculptures are in numerous collections including the MOMA, the Daum Museum, the LA County Museum of Art, the Miller Theater, the Museum of Contemporary Art, the Kyung-ju, and the Hermitage Museum, St. Petersburg.

Neil Forrest is an internationally exhibiting ceramic artist and professor at NSCAD University. He is involved in a multi-year research grant called 'Porøs,' in conjunction with The Oslo National Academy of the Arts. The project originates in the nature of clay itself – how porosity works as expressive instrument. Forrest received his Masters from Alfred University in New York, his BFA from Cranbrook Academy of Art in Michigan and diploma from Sheridan College of Craft.

Marty Augustyniak is a specialist in the design of membrane structures for the Façade Engineering practice at Walter P Moore. He developed a patented membrane product and manufacturing techniques that have become a standard in extreme climates. Martin is a licensed engineer in Florida, California and Nevada.

Mitchell Bring serves as an adjunct research Professor at the UB School of Architecture and Planning. He has been embedded at Boston Valley Terra Cotta to recruit and direct former students to assist with the company's digital transformation.

Flavio Borrelli is an Italian architect and self-taught artist dedicated to architectural research and experimentation in design by reinventing the approach to traditional materials and construction techniques. His work is currently dedicated to customize the architectural space with crafted expressiveness, searching for the reciprocal influences between art and architecture.

Cory Brugger is an architect and engineer who has worked with mOrphosis Architects Since 2010. He directs the development and application of innovative technology for design and construction and manages the implementation of advanced design technology for the firm's multidisciplinary project teams. Cory currently chairs the AIA's Technology in Architectural Practice (TAP) Knowledge Community committee.

Noah Burwell, is a Senior Associate with Walter P Moore. Some of Noah's notable projects include the Jockey Club Innovation Tower with Zaha Hadid Architects, Museum Plus with Herzog & de Meuron, and Terminal 3 at Taoyuan International Airport in Taipei with Rogers Stirk Harbour + Partners.

Graham Clegg is Associate Principal at STUDIOS Architecture New York City office where he is a leader of Building and Major Renovation Practices. Graham's focus is design and execution of large and complex projects. His accomplishments include the renovation of Kearny Point, a historic shipyard in

Kearny, NJ and many other LEED renovated historic structures.

Christine Dunn, AIA, Principal Architect at Sasaki, works across the disciplines of architecture, landscape and urban planning. Her practice focuses on projects within the arts, culture, and civic realms. Driven by the power of sensory and social human experiences in the built environment, Christine's work is inspired by ongoing research in digital design, fabrication and new material applications.

Laura Garófalo is an Associate Professor at the School of Architecture and Planning at Buffalo, and co-founder of Liminal Projects. Her work has received national and international design awards and been widely published and exhibited at multiple venues including the Architectural League of New York, the National Building Museum and Le Jardin De Metis.

Matt Gindlesparger is the Product Development Manager at AECOM and Assistant professor at Thomas Jefferson University. His research focuses on new technologies for the building industry. Recently, Matt has worked to develop, manufacture, and install a 700 square foot, building integrated, plant based bio-filtration system to improve air quality in the Public Safety Answering Center in the Bronx, NY.

Jason Green is an artist working with architectural terra cotta, tile and sculpture to explore intersections and opportunities found between pattern design, traditional processes and digital design and fabrication technologies. Green is a Visiting Assistant Professor at the New York State College of Ceramics in Alfred, NY.

Barry Ginder is a Senior Project Designer at Granum A/I. His work has been widely exhibited and recognized with numerous design awards including the John Stewardson Memorial Fellowship for Design Excellence and multiple AIA Awards for Design Excellence. Publications of his work include DWELL magazine, BUCKS Art + Culture Magazine, and the Philadelphia Inquirer.

Shay Harrison is the CEO of EcoCeramics Envelope Systems (EES), a collaboration with Jason Vollen (AECOM) focused on building façade energy management systems. He is materials scientist focused on the manufacturing of EES prototypes. EcoCeramics participated in the NEXUS-NY entrepreneur program at High Tech Rochester and has completed a GTAC project with RIT to improve modeling of the EES system performance.

Charles D. Jones is a Principal at One to One Design and serves as a faculty member at the Tulane School of Architecture. Previously, Charles worked with Gehry Partners LLP where he focused on the 3D development of complex exterior cladding assemblies including the Louis Vuitton Foundation in Paris, France.

Marco Juliani is currently a Job Captain at Gensler Architects. He formerly worked at Woods Baggot and Buttrick Projects Architecture + Design. He received his B.Arch from the University of Arizona.

Alexander Kellum, visual artist, recently received commissions for permanent art installations, curated by Peter Marino, at Christian Dior flagship stores in Seoul, Korea and Hong Kong, China. His work has been featured in Da Wang Gallery in Shenzhen, The Arch Gallery in Brooklyn, and the Lisa Dent Gallery in San Francisco.

Alex Korter, AIA, RIBA, LEED AP BD+C, is Associate Principal at CO Architects in Los Angeles, California. His architectural experience encompasses the oversight of projects varying in typology and complexity across Europe and the US. Alex is interested in developing innovative exterior envelopes and making sustainable design a fundamental part of all projects. While he is currently Project Architect on several buildings at CO Architects, he also leads their Building Facades Group.

Brett Laureys is a Principal with Wiss, Janney, Elstner, Associates, Inc. in Northbrook, Illinois. For the past 23 years, Brett has specialized in the evaluation and repair of historic buildings and structures.

His focus has been the assessment and restoration design for historic terra cotta clad buildings across the United States. His portfolio includes the restoration of multiple Louis Sullivan and Frank Lloyd Wright designed buildings.

Irene Martin is Senior Building Envelope Physicist at Arup. Her focus is energy efficiency, thermal comfort, resource use minimization, and thermal/solar performance as these relate to the building envelope. Irene co-authored Arup's Sustainable Façade Design Guide, has been a guest lecturer at SCI-Arc and USC, and teaches internal Arup course on Building Envelope Physics.

Heath May, AIA, is Associate Principal and Director of HKS Laboratory for INtensive Exploration. Heath focuses on computation, simulation and digital design and fabrication, with projects such as future GSA, a net-zero renovation solution that earned the 2012 WAN Commercial Building of the Year Award, and Sustainable Urban Living, a winner of the 2010 Chicago Athenaeum Green Good Design Award.

David Merlin, AIA, LEED-AP, is a Principal at One to One Design, a full service architecture firm that also provides consulting for artists, facade designers, and other design firms. Did is also an adjunct lecturer at Tulane School of Architecture. At One to One Design, he leads projects through all phases of design, and heads the computation design unit.

Shawn Murrey is an Adjunct Professor and Technical Specialist for the Ceramic Art Department at Alfred University. Shawn has exhibited his artwork nationally and internationally, most recently at the Burchfield Penny Art Museum in Buffalo, New York and The Cross Mackenzie Gallery in Washington, D.C.

Chris O'Hara is an Engineer and founding Principal of Studio NYL, a leading structural engineering firm known for its progressive approach to designing architectural structures. He leads the Skins Group, specializing in thermal modeling, moisture/condensation analysis, in-depth detailing and more. Prior to co-founding Studio NYL, O'Hara worked for a number of the world's prominent facade designers.

Zac Potts is a Designer at HKS and a Lecturer at the University of Texas at Arlington. Working in the HKS LINE Studio (Laboratory for INtensive Exploration) Zac helps research and develop the design process through the use of emerging technology. At the UTA, Zac explores the relationship of object and digital production.

Andrew Pries is a Production Manager at Boston Valley Terra Cotta. He earned his B.S. in Architecture from the University at Buffalo and his Master of Architecture from the University of Michigan. His current work and research focuses on how to augment digital tools with traditional craftsmanship to develop new workflows and increase production capacity.

Casey Reas is a media artist and co-creator of Processing programing language. He is a Professor of Design Media Arts at the University of California, LA. He has shown his work at the Whitney Museum of American Art's artport, the Ars Electronica, the ZKM, the GAFFTA, the Danish Film Institute, bitforms gallery, the IAMAS and ICC in Japan, and multiple art festivals.

Peter Schmidt manages Information Technology at Boston Valley Terra Cotta, where he has focused on 3D scanning, design for fabrication, and integrated database tracking. His award winning Masters thesis from the University at Buffalo resulted in the design of a 4-axis wire cutter to customize extruded terracotta for parametrically variable facades.

Joshua G. Stein is the co-director of the Data Clay Network, a forum for the exploration of digital techniques applied to ceramic materials, and the founder of Los Angeles-based studio Radical Craft. He was a 2010–11 Rome Prize Fellow in Architecture, and is currently Professor of Architecture at Woodbury University.

Matt Stephenson is a Senior Associate at Woods Bagot's New York studio. His responsibilities include directing the design process of multiple projects within the New York studio as well as coordinating with design teams and leaders from across 17 global studios to ensure the elevation of the firm's design.

Stan Su is the Director of Enclosure Design at Morphosis, serving as office-wide lead on façade technology and fabrication. He brings diverse experience to the firm having worked in both architectural design teams and facades-specific consultant teams. His guidance ensures that quality is upheld throughout the virtual design and construction process.

Erik Verboon is the Co-Founder and Managing Director of Walter P Moore's New York office. He focuses on the design of complex and high-performance building envelopes. His portfolio showcases both national and international work with extensive experience in the New York market. In addition, he teaches enclosure design at a number of leading universities.

Jason Vollen, AIA, is Principal and Director of High Performance Buildings at AECOM, Chief Operating Officer of Fresh Air Building Systems LLC, and cofounder of EcoCeramics Envelope Systems (EES), a collaboration focused on developing a ceramic-based energy transfer building envelope. Vollen's research has been funded by the NSF, DOE, NREL, NYSERDA and the AIA and he has won numerous awards for next generation building systems design and has multiple building system patents under review.

Kelly Winn, PhD, is a Lecturer at Rensselaer Polytechnic Institute and an Architectural Researcher with the Center for Architecture Science and Ecology (CASE). His work is focuses on computational design, environmental analysis, and climatically adapted architectural ceramic facades. Kelly has a PhD in Architectural Sciences from Rensselaer and a M.Arch from the University of Arizona.

Han Zhang is a Façade Engineer at Arup's Sydney Office. He has a remedial and diagnostic engineering role looking at cause and effect of building fabric failures and remediation strategies. He has worked on a number of significant building remediation and conservation projects including the Sydney Opera House, the former Sydney Water Board Building, Ski Dubai and Grosvenor Place.

Linda Zhang is the Boghosian Faculty Fellow at Syracuse University School of Architecture. She engages both theoretical and practical aspects of material processes to explore new forms of critical memory in architecture, most recently focusing on slip-casting. Her work has been exhibited internationally in Germany, Canada, the United States, Italy, Spain and Japan.

Glazing applied to extruded components at Boston Valley.

Adjustments needed to be made to the prototypes to better accommodate the assembly design, giving participants an understanding of
the tolerances required for terra-cotta components.

Several teams explored innovating the connections between the ceramic components and the rain screen track system.

Assembly of the unitized components helped both designers and engineers gain a greater understanding of the potentials of terracotta systems.

Acknowledgments

Boston Valley Terra Cotta

Boston Valley Terra Cotta was established by the Krouse family in 1981 following the purchase of Boston Valley Pottery. Utilizing both superior terra cotta engineering knowledge and sculpting talent, Boston Valley Terra Cotta has become one of the leading manufacturers of architectural terra cotta in the country. Boston Valley commenced operations with the restoration of Louis Sullivan's Guaranty Building. Since then, the company has been awarded contracts for some of the most notable buildings around the country. They have over 30 years of experience in design engineering, drafting, model and mold making, clay body and glaze development, and customer service. They operate a facility in Orchard Park, NY with 170,000 square feet of work space and over 150 employees.

The School of Architecture and Planning at the University at Buffalo (SUNY)

The UB School of Architecture and Planning was created in 1968 as a direct challenge to orthodox design education. It lives those original principles today, committed to architecture and planning as interdisciplinary problem-solving enterprises, rooted in social engagement, nourished by research-in-practice, animated by making and doing, and committed to meeting the needs of clients, communities, and society in an increasingly complex urban world.

Throughout nearly half a century of work, the people of the School of Architecture and Planning have grappled with how to make cities more livable and humane; how to conserve and produce energy within the urban fabric; how to make every environment more accessible to people of all abilities; and how to make all of the built environment more responsive to our human goals and protective of our increasingly fragile natural ecologies. In our early years, faculty were inspired by the insights of general systems theorists and the Bauhaus dream of a fusion of technology and art in service to society. Over the years, other intellectual traditions have made their mark on the life of the school. But some things have remained constant even as they have grown and flowered, namely a commitment to research, engaged work, and the values of urbanism.

University at Buffalo Sustainable Manufacturing and Advanced Robotic Technologies (SMART)

Building upon UB's reputation as a leader in advanced manufacturing and design, the Sustainable Manufacturing and Advanced Robotic Technologies (SMART) community will help create the next generation of technologies, processes and education. The SMART CoE is expected to impact scholarship, education, and engagement in eight interdisciplinary themes: Sustainable Design and Innovation, Humans-in-the-Loop, Materials and Materials Innovation, Information Processing, Advanced Design and Manufacturing, Transformative Design, Industry and Community partnerships and SMART education.

School of Art and Design and The Kazuo Inamori School of Engineering at The NYS College of Ceramics at Alfred University

The NYS College of Ceramics (NYSCC) is a statutory college of the State University of New York within Alfred University that includes the School of Art & Design and the Ceramic Engineering and Materials Science programs. NYSCC is renowned for its expertise in glass and ceramics. The Inamori School of Engineering is one of only two institutions in the U.S. that offer a B.S. in Ceramic Engineering, and the only institution in the U.S. that offers degrees in Glass Science. The School of Art and Design's M.F.A. programs are ranked by U.S. News and World report among the top eleven programs overall. The college's focus on glass and ceramics is further expressed in the activities of the Inamori-Kyocera Fine Ceramics Museum, the Alfred Ceramic Art Museum, and the NYS Center for Advanced Ceramic Technology.

Participants were also provided with green-ware so they could make alterations to the units to improve the design.

The Morphosis team sketching solutions for assembling the terracotta panels.

At Boston Valley, teams saw the variety of applications for this versatile material with historic restoration and contemporary rain screen panels produced through similar techniques.